TEXTURED CROCHET LACE

**64 crochet lace patterns
to create
rugs, scarves, beanies
and more**

RENATE KIRKPATRICK

SALLY MILNER PUBLISHING

First published in 2012 by
Sally Milner Publishing Pty Ltd
734 Woodville Road
Binda NSW 2583 AUSTRALIA

© Renate Kirkpatrick 2012

Design: Anna Warren, Warren Ventures Pty Ltd
Editing: Anne Savage
Photography: Tim Connolly

Printed in China

National Library of Australia Cataloguing-in-Publication entry

Author: Kirkpatrick, Renate, 1951-
Title: Textured crochet lace : 64 lace patterns to create rugs, scarves,
                 beanies and more / Renate Kirkpatrick.
ISBN: 9781863514309 (pbk.)
Series: Milner craft series.
Subjects: Crocheting--Patterns.
Dewey Number: 746.434041

Disclaimer
Information and instructions given in this book are presented in good faith, but no
warranty is given nor results guaranteed, nor is freedom from any patent to be inferred. As
we have no control over physical conditions surrounding application of information herein
contained in this book, the author and publisher disclaim any liability for untoward results.

10 9 8 7 6 5 4 3 2 1

Acknowledgements

My heartfelt thanks:

⟡ to my family and friends who patiently endure my many yarn adventures even when they haven't a clue to what I'm on about ...

⟡ to my wonderful, loyal and steadfast students who turn up to class no matter what ... rain, hail or shine. Together we've learnt so much.

⟡ to the many, many crafty online friends that I've come to know across cyberspace, for your help and inspiration.

⟡ to Libby Renney and her staff at Sally Milner Publishing for, once again, taking me on.

Requirements for 64-pattern textured lace sampler in photo:

Bendigo Woollen Mills Classic 8-ply yarn (100% pure wool)

Col A: 700 g Periwinkle 600 (blue)

Col B: 650 g Sweet Pea 705 (pink)

Col C: 650 g Blueberry 704 (purple)

Col D: 250 g Ensign 667 (navy): joining squares and borders

Crochet hook size 5.00 (H)

The completed 64-pattern textured lace sampler

The aim of this book

My aim with this book has been to bring together a collection
of interesting crochet lace patterns than can be worked into
your general crochet repertoire and increase your crochet
knowledge, confidence and pleasure. Work your way through
all 64 patterns and you will have a beautiful rug (an afghan)
that will take pride of place in your home—choose a collection
of favourite patterns and create your own smaller rug for that
special person in your life or just choose one pattern for a scarf
or shawl in your yarn of choice. I enjoy incorporating many of
these patterns into to my freestyle/freeform work and my hope
is that many of you, as your skills grow, will venture out and
do the same … after all, we are really only limited by our own
imagination … enjoy!

Dedication

To all crochet diehards—your endless interest and enthusiasm
has brought this wonderful versatile craft back to life and help
to keep it vital and flourishing.

Contents

Introduction: why another sampler rug?

I will always be a great advocate of the sampler rug (afghan). Aside from being an excellent teaching and learning tool, the project itself becomes a practical goal-setter. As with my previous samplers, *Textured Crochet Lace* is a collection of stitch patterns ranging from the familiar for the less experienced, to the challenging for the more experienced. Utilising all the patterns will result in a rug approximately 152 cm (60 in) square, but there is no reason why you can't choose a selection of favourites (say 30 to 36 squares) for a smaller knee rug—either way, by working your way through the assortment of stitch patterns you are not only increasing your crochet repertoire and inadvertently gathering confidence but you also achieve that wonderful feeling of satisfaction that comes with the accomplishment of a job well done—a functional rug to show off to one and all—a beautiful heirloom that can be proudly passed down the generations.

Moreover, these patterns are so versatile that I've used them over and over again, for scarves, shawls, beanies and vests. I've even incorporated them into my lacy freeform/freestyle work.

Crochet fundamentals

I've included the following crochet fundamentals to refresh the memory and help you on your way of bringing open weave texture into your work—enjoy.

Bits and pieces you'll need

- A collection of yarn for swatches to try out unfamiliar stitches
- Blunt darning needle for sewing in tail-ends
- Scissors
- Rust-proof pins
- Safety pins, markers, short lengths of yarn (for markers)
- Tape measure

Reading patterns

Sometimes crochet patterns can be rather wordy, particularly circular motifs that require instruction for each round—this can be a daunting experience, especially for the beginner. My advice is to glance through the pattern and see if there's anything unusual that you need to know, then go back to the beginning and follow the pattern from one comma to the next comma. Everything between those commas is one instruction. For example: 1 ch, dc (US sc) in next 3 sts—make the 1 ch, then work a dc (US sc) in each of the next 3 stitches, and so on. Don't be frightened by the terminology and symbols; you'll soon be familiar with what, to the newcomer, looks like another language. Above all, take your time. If you come across a particularly complicated section and you're having trouble nutting it out, put your work aside for the minute, make yourself a cuppa and take a deep breath. Then, have another go—you'll often find it's not nearly as complicated as you first thought.

And I strongly suggest making use of both the written patterns and diagrams. You will be surprised how much clearer the instructions become.

Markers

In the past I considered markers a needless interruption to the job at hand and rarely used them. Then, a particularly complicated project came along where markers were essential, and I suddenly realised how helpful they really are. The small amount of time it takes to place them saves hours in the long run and I have used them ever since. I use markers to indicate right side or top/bottom of work, first stitch of round, centre stitches in corners and my crocheting life has never been easier. Commercial markers can be purchased from any craft supplier but safety pins or short yarn off-cuts (which I use) do the job just as well.

Yarn

My advice is to always to use yarn you like working with (but preferably the same ply as the pattern recommends). I'm not a purist and never shy away from using economy yarn if a colour and/or texture is right for a particular project. Later, when you've gained experience and grown in confidence you may decide to spend a little more on your yarn. Remember to purchase enough of the dye lot to complete your project. It's always better to have a little too much than to run out with two motifs to go. It's also a good idea to keep yarn labels as reference so that, if a dye lot has run out wherever you purchased it, you can contact the manufacturer.

Swatches

Being usually in too much of a hurry getting on with the project in hand, I've never really been a great advocate for making swatches (unless it's a garment where size is an issue). However, *Textured Crochet Lace* does include a couple of tricky patterns that would benefit from being worked out beforehand using some scrap yarn and thereby saving wear and tear on the better yarn I presume you would be working with.

Pattern difficulty differs from person to person; what is easy for one may seem complicated to another, therefore

I suggest using your discretion as to when to work a swatch. If the pattern looks more intricate than you're used to or you come across an unfamiliar stitch, it's worth the effort to nut it out before hand.

Tension

The size given earlier for the completed rug, approximately 152 cm (60 in) square, is only a guide—how loosely or tightly you crochet and the size of the hook you use will both influence the dimensions of your rug but the overall difference isn't vital. The hook size and yarns suggested are recommendations rather than precise specifications. It's far more important that your work is consistent, something that is much easier to achieve if you're working within your own comfort zone. This is your project; work with the hook size, colours and yarns you prefer. Enjoyment, knowledge and confidence are the aim—not trying to reproduce exactly the same rug, either in size or colour, as mine.

A helpful tip for keeping yarn flowing freely is taking it from the centre of the ball. This way the yarn comes to you and not the other way round

Determining square size

From time to time fold your square corner to corner to determine how many rows will be required before the top corners meet. When coming to the end of the square try ending with the row most similar to the first row. For example, if the first row was worked in dc (US sc), finish on a row of dc (US sc) also.

Edging

When edging your squares (or motifs) it is imperative that you work the number of stitches stated in the pattern (three stitches in corners and a certain number of stitches between). The top and bottom edges are usually straightforward. It's the two side edges that sometimes pose a bit of a problem because there are no obvious stitches to work. Nevertheless, it's important that the same number of stitches is worked along these sides—even though you may feel that they are being squeezed in or are too far apart. Just work as neatly and evenly as you can. The reason will become clear later when you are joining your squares (or motifs) stitch for stitch.

Tips for an attractive finish

It would be a real shame to have your project spoiled by an unsightly overall finish after spending many diligent hours working out the patterns.

In my experience the most common mistakes made in crochet are at the beginning and end of rows due to the confusion as to where to work the first and last stitch. If your work has uneven edges that zigzag here and there, or it leans off to one side, there's a good chance this fundamental is being overlooked. I hope the following Guide to crochet stitches and techniques will help remedy this frustrating problem.

Guide to crochet stitches and techniques

The *foundation chain* refers to the number of chains required for the length and/or pattern plus the extra chains that are required to accommodate the height of stitch in the row about to be worked. For example: if trebles (US double crochet) are being used you will need 2 extra chains for the foundation chain and 3 extra chains on each working row.

These 3 extra chains are called the *turning chain* (or *beginning chain*) and unless the pattern states otherwise must always counted as the *first stitch* of the row or round. This means that in subsequent rows or rounds the turning chain must be treated as a stitch at the end of each previous row or round.

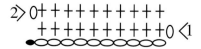

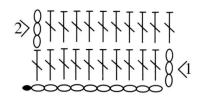

Where to work the first stitch?

For double crochet (US single crochet)/ dc (US sc), insert hook in first stitch to start new row:

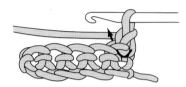

For all tall posted stitches, insert hook in second stitch to start new row. The example shows trebles (US double crochet)/tr (US dc):

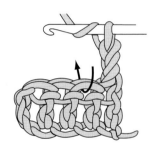

Joining new yarn and dealing with tail ends

I personally don't like using knots to join in new yarn. They produce weak spots and have the annoying habit of moving to the front of your work and spoiling all your hard-earned results.

My advice for avoiding the use of knots is to use one of the following two methods, which are standard recommendations for the neatest ways of bringing in new yarn, and apply whether changing colour or just bringing in new yarn as the current ball runs out.

1   Place new yarn along the top of your work and crochet a few stitches over it before the old yarn runs out; then pick up the new and crochet over the old:

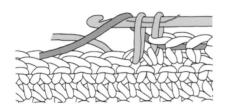

2   When 2 loops of the last stitch remain on hook, drop old yarn, pick up new yarn and draw through 2 loops:

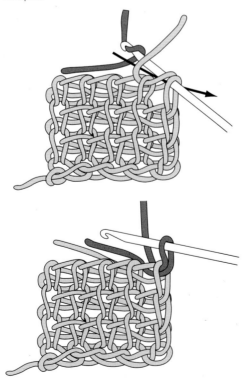

Another common problem relates to the false economy of leaving short tail-ends. Leave tail-ends of a reasonable length that can be easily and securely woven in later with a blunt darning needle—nothing spoils your work more than fluffy ends popping up. Better still, wherever possible crochet over the ends as you work—this saves on that big job at the end.

Blocking

As a general rule, I do not block sampler squares or motifs unless it's absolutely necessary. As your pile of completed squares begins to grow, you may become concerned by their slight variation in size and feel the need to block them to size. This variation is due to the variety of stitch patterns used in the samplers, and blocking is certainly one way of bringing them into line. However, and I can't stress this enough (you have to trust me here), if the correct number of stitches has been worked around the edges, blocking becomes an unnecessary exercise. Later you will be joining the squares stitch for stitch, which naturally brings them together. I also advise draping the finished rug over the back of a sofa for a week or so and letting it drop into shape. If by chance you find a square exceedingly out of line with the rest it may be worth making it again, using a smaller or larger hook depending on whether the square is too big or too small.

Methods for those who want to block:

1 Place the squares on a terry towel over a flat surface and, using rust-proof pins, secure them to shape, lightly steam and allow to dry completely. Be aware that the heat and steam can sometimes weaken the body fibre of some yarns and flatten textured stitches.

2 I prefer this method for its lesser degree of interference with the yarn's body fibre and for retaining textured stitches: secure squares as above, then apply spray starch liberally and allow to dry completely.

Using the placement chart

This placement chart is a guide only. When different colours have been used you may need to move the squares around to achieve the most pleasing colour arrangement.

12	54	31	7	47	32	4	61
41	17	51	28	6	44	27	8
46	40	13	53	23	9	55	26
11	60	42	5	52	29	2	58
30	18	59	34	16	48	25	10
63	39	1	57	43	3	49	24
22	64	38	19	45	33	20	50
35	14	62	37	21	56	36	15

Joining individual squares

Lay out squares according to the placement chart or in the order you prefer and pin themtogether. For ease of handling work with just two rows at a time. Take care to always join the rows from the same end.

Working from right to left, with right sides of both squares facing outward, work back loop (centre loops) of both squares, joining in first sts using one of the joining techniques listed below.

1 **Invisible join using mattress stitch (ladder st):** with right side facing, lay squares or motif to be joined side-by-side on a flat surface and with a blunt darning needle join in back loop of one square:
    - slide the needle through two loops of second square, then two loops of the first again
    - repeat a couple of times and draw together firmly
    - ease the stitches back gently with your fingers
    - continue until the join is complete
    - weave in ends.

2 **Visible or flat join using whip stitch:** with the wrong sides of the squares facing and using a blunt darning needle, overcast stitch each corresponding st together to end. Weave in ends.

3 **SS join:** with right sides facing, join with ss in first sts and ss each corresponding st together to end. Weave in ends.

4 **Dc (US sc) join:** with right side facing, join with dc (US sc) in first sts, dc (US sc) each corresponding st together to end. Weave in ends. This method, which is the strongest, was used for the sampler in the photograph.

All-round border edging (when all squares are joined)

Round 1: (for this round work in back loops only) with right side facing, join Col D (edging colour) with dc (US sc) in back loop of any corner st, work 2 dc (US sc) in same st, *dc (US sc) in each st to next corner st, 3 dc (US sc) in corner st, repeat from * around join with ss to first dc (US sc), do not finish off.

Round 2: (from now on work in both loops) continuing with Col D, 1 ch, *dc (US sc) in same st and in each st across to next corner st, 3 dc (US sc) in next corner st, repeat from * around, join with ss to first dc (US sc), do not finish off.

Round 3: continuing with Col D, 1 ch, dc (US sc) in same st, *5 ch, skip next 3 corner sts, work dc in next st, 3 ch, skip 3 sts, repeat from * around, join with ss to first dc (US sc), do not finish off.

Round 4: continuing with Col D, *7 dc (US sc) in next 5-ch corner loop, ss in next dc, 5 dc (US sc) in next 3-ch loop and in each 3-ch loop to next 5-ch corner loop, repeat from * around, join with ss to first ss, finish off.

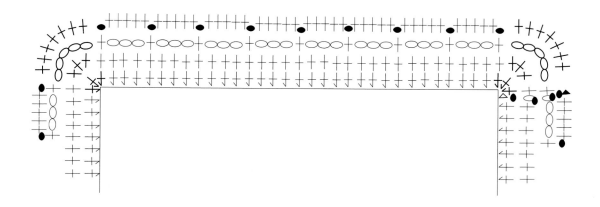

Basic crochet stitches: the following are standard stitch guides—variations are explained further in individual patterns where required.

Stitch guide	Abbreviations	
●	ss	slip stitch
○	ch	chain
+	dc (US sc)	double crochet (US single crochet)
T	htr (US hdc)	half treble (US half double crochet)
⌧	tr (US dc)	treble (US double crochet)
⌧	Ltr (US Ldc)	long treble (US long double crochet
⌧	dtr (US tr)	double treble (US treble)
	FP	front post
	BP	back post
	YO	yarn over

Slip knot

Use slip knots rather than just tying an ordinary knot—it's neater and allows the next chain (ch 1) to flow rather than being tugged through the loop just made. Never count the loop (on hook) as a chain or stitch.

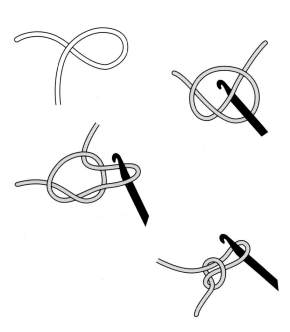

Slip stitch/ss

Insert hook into st, YO and draw yarn through st and loop on hook.

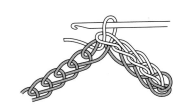

Double crochet/dc
(US single crochet/sc)

Working along foundation ch, insert hook into 2nd ch from hook, YO and draw loop through st (2 loops on hook), YO and draw yarn through both loops— dc (US sc) made.

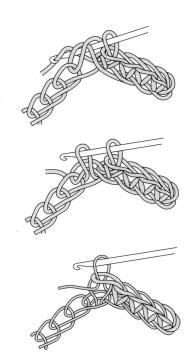

Foundation chain/chain/ch

The number of chains required for length and/or pattern plus the extra chains that are required to accommodate the stitch height.

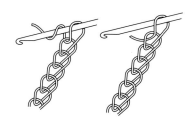

Half treble/htr
(US half double crochet/hdc)

Working along foundation ch, YO, insert hook into 3rd ch from hook, YO and draw loop through st (3 loops on hook), YO and draw yarn through all 3 loops—htr (US hdc) made.

Treble/tr
(US double crochet/dc)

Working along foundation ch, YO, insert hook into 4th ch from hook, YO and draw yarn through st (3 loops on hook), YO, draw through 2 loops, YO and draw through last 2 loops—tr (US dc) made.

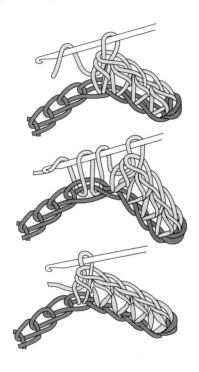

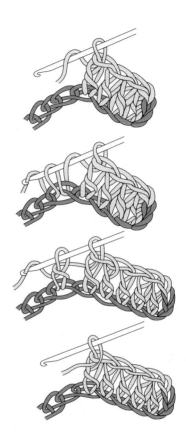

Double treble/dtr
(US treble crochet/tr)

YO twice, insert hook in st or sp and pull up a loop, YO and draw through 2 loops on hook 3 times.

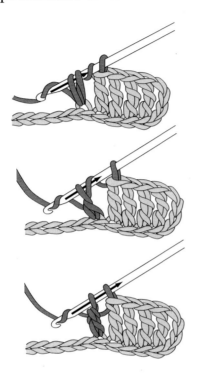

Front or back loop only

Work only in loop indicated by arrow.

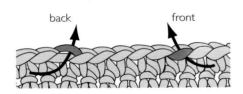

Post stitch (FP or BP)

Work around post of stitch indicated in row or rows below, inserting hook in direction of arrow.

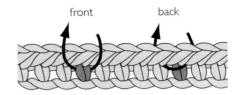

Beginning cluster

3ch, (YO, insert hook in ring and pull up a loop, YO and draw through 2 loops on hook) twice, YO and draw through all 3 loops on hook.

Cluster

YO, insert hook in stitch or space and pull up a loop, YO and draw through 2 loops on hook) 3 times, YO and draw through all 4 loops on hook

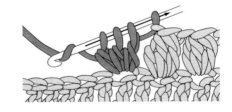

Popcorn

Work 5 tr or htr in st or sp, *drop loop from hook, insert hook in first st of group, **hook dropped loop and draw through, 1 ch to close.

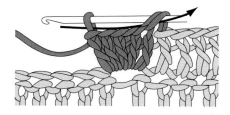

[whfb] = work hook from back

Work popcorn as usual to *, insert hook in first st of group from the back, then complete stitch from ** as for usual popcorn.

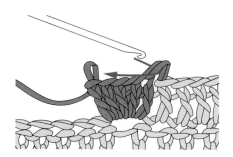

Puff stitch

(YO, insert hook in st or space, YO and pull up a loop even with hook) 3 or 4 times, YO and draw through all 7 or 9 loops on hook, 1 ch to close.

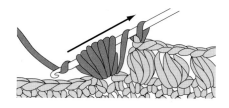

Finishing off (casting off stitch)

With the last stitch complete, cut yarn and draw through the loop on hook, pull tight to close the loop. Weave in end. With slippery yarn, draw through the loop twice (make an extra chain) and pull down very tightly with your thumb to close. Weave in end.

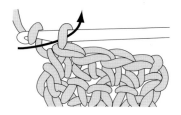

Symbols used in diagrams

◄ = finish off

◁ = bring in new yarn

〈   〉 = row turn

● = slip stitch/ss

○ = chain/ch

+ = double crochet/dc
(US single crochet/sc)

T = half treble/htr
(US half double crochet/hdc)

= treble/tr (US double crochet/dc)

= long treble/Ltr
(US long double crochet/Ldc)

= double treble/dtr (US treble/tr)

 = picot double treble cluster/picot dtr CL
(US picot treble cluster/picot tr CL)

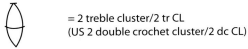
    a   b   c   d   e = cluster/CL

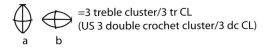 = 2 treble cluster/2 tr CL
(US 2 double crochet cluster/2 dc CL)

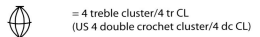
    a   b = 3 treble cluster/3 tr CL
(US 3 double crochet cluster/3 dc CL)

 = 4 treble cluster/4 tr CL
(US 4 double crochet cluster/4 dc CL)

work in front loops
    a   b   c = work in front loops

work in back loops
    a   b   c = work in back loops

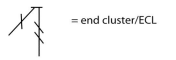 = front post double cluster/FPDCL

= front post/FPtr/FPhtr/
FPCL (US FPdc/FPhdc/FPCL)
    a   b   c   d   e

 = beginning cluster/BCL

= back post/BPtr/BPhtr
(US Bpdc/BPhdc)
    a   b   c   d   e

 = end cluster/ECL

= 4 tr popcorn (US 4 dc popcorn)

= 5 tr popcorn (US 5 dc popcorn)

= puff st

= picot/s
    a   b

= slant st

SIXTY FOUR TEXTURED LACE SQUARES

COLOUR GROUP A

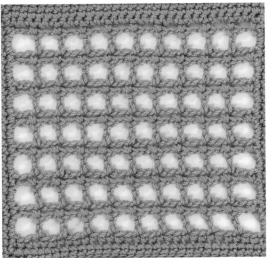

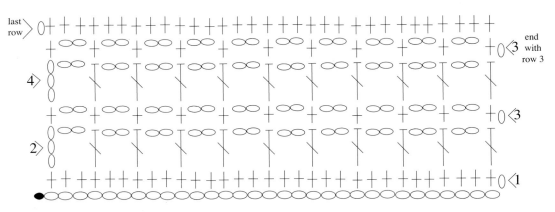

Foundation chain: With Col A make 32 ch.

Row 1: (right side) dc (US sc) in 2nd ch from hook and in each ch across—31 dc (US sc).

Row 2: 5 ch [count as tr (US dc) + 2 ch, now and throughout, beginning chain], turn, *skip next 2 sts, tr (US dc) in next st, 2 ch, repeat from * across—11 x tr (US dc) + 10 x 2-ch sps.

Row 3: 1 ch, turn, dc (US sc) in first st, *2 ch, skip next 2-ch sp, dc (US sc) in next st, repeat from * across to beginning chain, dc (US sc) in 3rd ch of beginning chain—11 x dc (US sc) + 10 x 2-ch sps.

Row 4: 5 ch, turn, *skip next 2-ch sp, tr (US dc) in next st, 2 ch, repeat from * across—11 x tr (US dc) + 10 x 2-ch sps.

Subsequent rows: repeat rows 2 and 3 to desired size ending with row 2, then work 1 last row as follows.

Last row: 1 ch, turn, dc (US sc) in each st and 2 dc (US sc) in each 2-ch sp across—do not finish off—work 2 rounds of edging in working colour before finishing off.

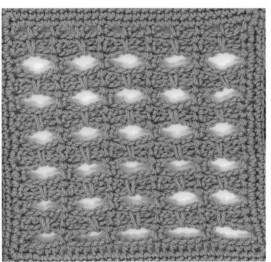

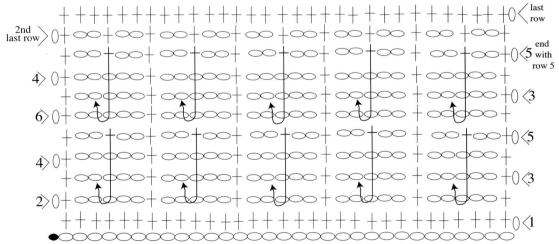

Foundation chain: With Col A make 32 ch.

Row 1: (right side) dc (US sc) in 2nd ch from hook and in each ch across—31 dc (US sc).

Row 2: 1 ch, turn, dc (US sc) in first st, *5 ch, skip 5 sts, dc (US sc) in next st, repeat from * across—5 x 5-ch sps.

Rows 3 and 4: 1 ch, turn, dc (US sc) in first st, *5 ch, skip next 5-ch loop, dc (US sc) in next st, repeat from * across—6 x dc (US sc) + 5 x 5-ch sps.

Row 5: 1 ch, turn, dc (US sc) in first st, *2 ch, work dc (US sc) around all 3 5-ch loops of previous 3 rows, 2 ch, dc (US sc) in next dc (US sc), repeat from * across—11 x dc (US sc) + 10 x 2-ch sps.

Row 6: 1 ch, turn, dc (US sc) in first st, *5 ch, skip next dc (US sc), dc (US sc) in next dc (US sc), repeat from * across—5 x 5-ch sps.

Rows 7 and 8: repeat rows 3 and 4.

Subsequent rows: repeat rows 3 to 6 to desired size ending with row 5, then work 2 last rows as follows.

2nd last row: 1 ch, turn, dc (US sc) in first st, *2 ch, dc (US sc) in next dc (US sc), repeat from * across—11 x dc (US sc) + 10 x 2-ch sps.

Last row: 1 ch, turn, dc (US sc) in each st and 2 dc (US sc) in each 2-ch sp across—do not finish off—work 2 rounds of edging in working colour before finishing off.

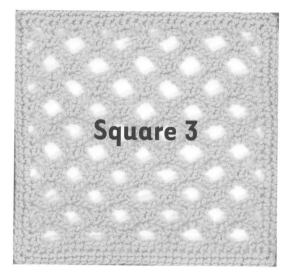

Square 3

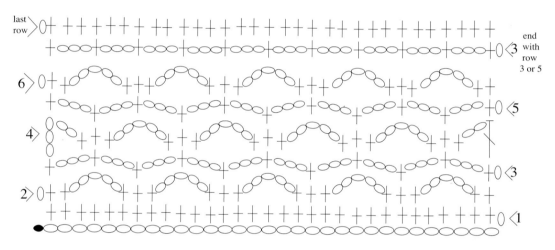

Foundation chain: With Col A make 32 ch.

Row 1: (right side) dc (US sc) in 2nd ch from hook and in each ch across—31 dc (US sc).

Row 2: 1 ch, turn, dc (US sc) in first 2 sts, *5 ch, skip next 3 sts, dc (US sc) in each next 3 sts, repeat from * across to last 2 sts, dc (US sc) in last 2 sts—5 x 5-ch sps.

Row 3: 1 ch, turn, dc (US sc) in first st, *3 ch, dc (US sc) in next 5-ch sp, 3 ch, dc (US sc) in 2nd st of next 3-dc (US sc) group, repeat from * across ending with dc (US sc) in last st—10 x 3-ch sps.

Row 4: 5 ch (count as tr + 2 ch, now and throughout, beginning chain), turn, *skip next 2 ch, dc (US sc) in next ch, dc (US sc) in next dc (US sc), dc (US sc) in next ch, 5 ch, skip next (2 ch + next dc (US sc)), repeat from * across ending with 2 ch, skip 2 ch, tr in last st—4 x 5-ch sps + 2 x 2-ch sps.

Row 5: 1 ch, turn, dc (US sc) in first st, *3 ch, dc (US sc) in 2nd st of next 3-dc (US sc) group, 3 ch, dc (US sc) in next 5-ch sp, repeat from * across to beginning chain, dc (US sc) in 3rd ch of beginning chain—10 x 3-ch sps.

Row 6: 1 ch, turn, dc (US sc) in first st and in next ch, *5 ch, skip next (2-ch sp, next dc (US sc) and next 2 ch), dc (US

sc) in next ch, dc (US sc) in next st, dc (US sc) in next ch, repeat from * across ending with, dc (US sc) in last ch and last st—5 x 5-ch sps.

Subsequent rows: repeat rows 3 to 6 to desired size ending with row 3 or 5, then work 1 last row as follows.

Last row: 1 ch, turn, dc (US sc) in each st and 2 dc in each 3-ch sp across—do not finish off—work 2 rounds of edging in working colour before finishing off.

Square 4

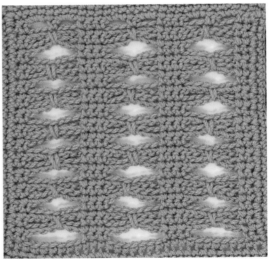

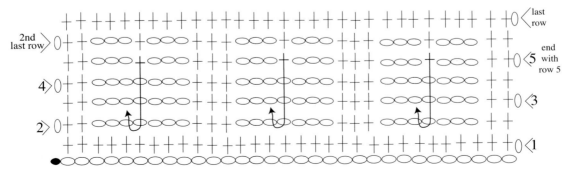

Foundation chain: With Col A make 32 ch.

Row 1: (right side) dc (US sc) in 2nd ch from hook and in each ch across—31 dc (US sc).

Row 2: 1 ch, turn, dc (US sc) in first 2 sts, *7 ch, skip 7 sts, dc (US sc) in each next 3 sts, repeat from * across to last 2 sts, dc (US sc) in each last 2 sts—3 x 7-ch loops.

Row 3 and 4: ch, turn, dc (US sc) in first 2 sts, *7 ch, skip 7-ch sp, dc (US sc) in each next 3 sts, repeat from * across ending with dc (US sc) in each last 2 sts—3 x 7-ch loops.

Row 5: 1 ch, turn, dc (US sc) in first 2 sts, *3 ch, work dc (US sc) around all 3 7-ch loops of previous 3 rows, 3 ch, dc (US sc) in each next 3 sts, repeat from * across ending with dc (US sc) in each last 2 sts—6 x 3-ch loops.

Row 6: ch, turn, dc (US sc) in first 2 sts, *7 ch, skip next 3-ch sp, dc (US sc) and next 3-ch sp, dc (US sc) in next 3 sts, repeat from * across ending with dc (US sc) in each last 2 sts—3 x 7-ch loops.

Subsequent rows: repeat rows 3 to 6 to desired size ending with row 5, then work 2 last rows as follows.

2nd last row: 1 ch, turn, dc (US sc) in first 2 sts, *3 ch, dc (US sc) in next dc (US sc), 3 ch, dc (US sc) in each next 3 sts, repeat from * across ending with dc (US sc) in each last 2 sts—6 x 3-ch loops.

Last row: 1 ch, turn, dc (US sc) in each st and 3 dc (US sc) in each 3-ch sp across—do not finish off—work 2 rounds of edging in working colour before finishing off.

Square 5

Foundation chain: With Col A make 32 ch.

Row 1: (right side) dc (US sc) in 2nd ch from hook and in each ch across—31 dc (US sc).

Row 2: 3 ch [count as tr (US dc) now and throughout, beginning chain], turn, tr (US dc) in next 2 sts, *4 ch, skip 2 sts, work (dtr (US tr) in next st, skip next st) 3 times, dtr (US tr) in next st, 4 ch, skip 2 sts, tr (US dc) in each next 3 sts, repeat from * across—9 x tr (US dc) + 8 x dtr (US tr) + 4 x 4-ch sps.

Row 3: 3 ch, turn tr (US dc) in next 2 sts, *4 ch, skip 4-ch sp, dc (US sc) in each next 4 sts, 4 ch, skip 4-ch sp, tr (US dc) in each next 3 sts, repeat from * across—9 x tr (US dc) + 8 x dc (US sc) + 4 x 4-ch sps.

Row 4 and 5: repeat row 3.

Row 6: 3 ch, turn, tr (US dc) in next 2 sts, *2 ch, skip 4-ch sp, work (dtr (US tr) in next st, 1 ch) 3 times, dtr (US tr) in next st, 2 ch, tr (US dc) in next 3 sts, repeat from * across—9 x tr (US dc) + 8 x dtr (US tr) + 4 x 2-ch sps.

Row 7: 1 ch, turn, dc (US sc) in each st and 1-ch sp, 2 dc (US sc) in each 2-ch sp across—31 dc (US sc).

Row 8: 4 ch [count as tr (US dc) + 1 ch, beginning chain], turn, *skip next st, 1 ch, tr (US dc) in next st, repeat from * across—16 x tr (US dc) + 15 x 1-ch sps.

Row 9: 4 ch [count as tr (US dc) + 1 ch, beginning chain], turn, *skip next 1-ch sp, 1 ch, tr (US dc) in next st, repeat from * across—16 x tr (US dc) + 15 x 1-ch sps.

Row 10: 1 ch, turn, dc (US sc) in each st and 1-ch sp across—31 dc (US sc).

Subsequent rows: repeat rows 2 to 7 once more—do not finish off—work 2 rounds of edging in working colour before finishing off.

Double treble/dtr (US treble tr): YO twice, insert hook in st or sp and pull up a loop, YO and draw through 2 loops on hook 3 times.

Square 6

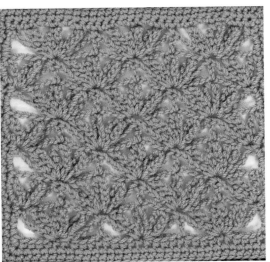

Foundation chain: With Col A make 32 ch.

Row 1: (right side) dc (US sc) in 2nd ch from hook and in each ch across—31 dc (US sc).

Row 2: 7 ch [count as tr (US dc) +4 ch, now and throughout, beginning chain], turn, *skip next 4 sts, in next st work [(dc (US sc), 7 ch) 3 times, dc (US sc), 4 ch], skip next 4 sts, tr (US dc) in next st, 4 ch, repeat from * across—9 x 7-ch loops.

Row 3: 1 ch, turn, dc (US sc) in first st, *1 ch, work [dc (US sc), 3 ch, in next 7-ch loop] twice, dc (US sc) in next 7-ch loop, 1 ch, dc (US sc) in next tr (US dc), repeat from * across to Beginning chain, dc (US sc) in 3rd ch of beginning chain—6 x 3-ch sps.

Row 4: turn, in first st work [7 ch, dc (US sc)] twice, 4 ch, *[skip next 1-ch sp, dc (US sc) and 3-ch sp], tr (US dc) in next st, 4 ch, skip next [3-ch sp, dc (US sc) and 1-ch sp], in next st work [(dc (US sc), 7 ch) 3 times, dc (US sc), 4 ch] repeat from * across to last st, in last st work [dc (US sc), 7 ch, dc (US sc), 4 ch, tr (US dc)] [count 4 ch and tr (US dc) just made as 7-ch loop]—10 x 7-ch loops.

Row 5: 1 ch, turn, dc (US sc) in first 7-ch loop, 3 ch, dc (US sc) in next 7-ch loop, *1 ch, dc (US sc) in next tr (US dc), 1 ch, dc (US sc) in next 7-ch loop, work [3 ch, dc (US sc) in next 7-ch loop] twice, repeat from * across to last 2 7-ch loops, in 2nd last 7-ch loop work [dc (US sc), 3 ch] and dc (US sc) in last 7-ch loop—13 x dc (US sc) + 6 x 3-ch loops.

Row 6: 7 ch, turn, *skip next [3-ch sp, dc (US sc) and 1-ch sp], in next st work [(dc (US sc), 7 ch) 3 times, dc (US sc), 4 ch], skip next [1-ch sp, dc (US sc) and 3-ch sp], tr (US dc) in next st, 4 ch, repeat from * across ending with tr (US dc) in last st—9 x 7-ch loops.

Subsequent rows: repeat rows 3 to 6 to desired size ending with row 3 or 5, then work 1 last row as follows.

Last row: 1 ch, turn, dc (US sc) in each st and 1-ch sp, and 2 dc (US sc) in each 3-ch sp—do not finish off—work 2 rounds of edging in working colour before finishing off.

Square 7

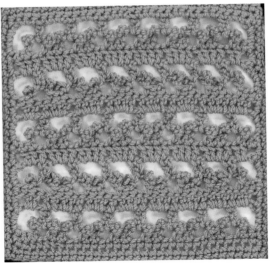

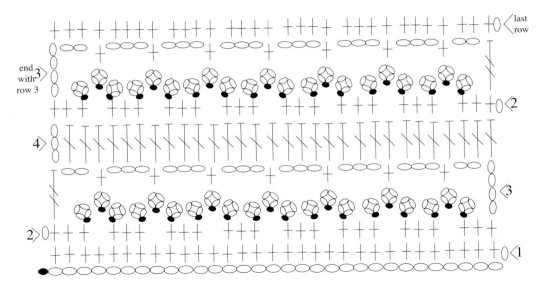

Foundation chain: With Col A make 32 ch.

Row 1: (right side) dc (US sc) in 2nd ch from hook and in each ch across—31 dc (US sc).

Row 2: 1 ch, turn, dc (US sc) in first 3 sts, *work 3 picots, skip next st, dc (US sc) in each next 3 sts, repeat from * across—21 x picots.

Row 3: 6 ch [count as dtr (US tr) + 2-ch sp, now and throughout, beginning chain], turn, *dc (US sc) in 2nd picot of next picot-group, 3 ch, repeat from *across ending with 2 ch and dtr (US tr) in last st—2 x dtr (US tr) + 6 x 3-ch sps + 2 x 2-ch sps.

Row 4: 3 ch [count as tr (US dc), now and throughout, beginning chain], turn, 2 tr (US dc) in next 2-ch sp, *tr (US dc) in next dc (US sc), 3 tr (US dc) in next 3-ch sp, repeat from * across ending with 2 tr (US dc) in last 2-ch sp and tr (US dc) in 3rd ch of beginning chain—31 x tr (US dc).

Subsequent rows: repeat rows 2 to 4 to desired size ending with row 3, then work last row as follows.

Last row: 1 ch, turn, dc (US sc) in each st, 2 dc (US sc) in each 2-ch sp and 3 dc (US sc) in each 3-ch sp across—do not finish off—work 2 rounds of edging in working colour before finishing off.

Picot: 4 ch, ss in 4th ch from hook (for best results work picot tightly).

Double treble/dtr (US treble/tr): YO twice, insert hook in st or sp and pull up a loop, YO and draw through 2 loops on hook 3 times.

Square 8

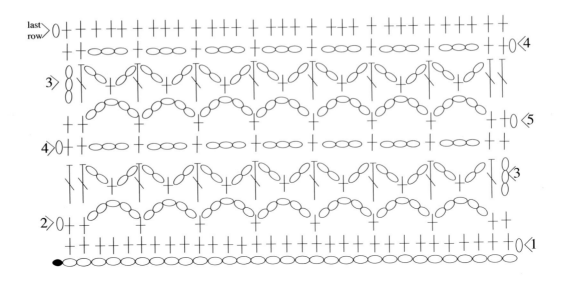

Foundation chain: With Col A make 32 ch.

Row 1: (right side) dc (US sc) in 2nd ch from hook and in each ch across—31 dc (US sc).

Row 2: 1 ch, turn, dc (US sc) in first 2 sts, *5 ch, skip 3 next sts, dc (US sc) in next st, repeat from * across ending with dc (US sc) in last st—7 x 5-ch sps.

Row 3: 3 ch [count as tr (US dc) now and throughout, beginning chain], turn, tr (US dc) in next st, *2 ch, dc (US sc) in next 5-ch sp, 2 ch, tr (US dc) in next st, repeat from * across ending with tr (US dc) in last st—14 x 2-ch sps.

Row 4: 1 ch, turn, dc (US sc) in first 2 sts, *3 ch, dc (US sc) in next tr (US dc), repeat from * across ending with dc (US sc) in last st—7 x 3-ch sps.

Row 5: 1 ch, turn, dc (US sc) in first 2 sts, *5 ch, dc (US sc) in next st, repeat from * across ending with dc (US sc) in last st—7 x 5-ch sps.

Subsequent rows: repeat rows 3 to 5 to desired size ending with row 4, then work 1 last row as follows.

Last row: 1 ch, turn, dc (US sc) in each st and 3 dc (US sc) in each 3-ch sp across—do not finish off—work 2 rounds of edging in working colour before finishing off.

Square 9

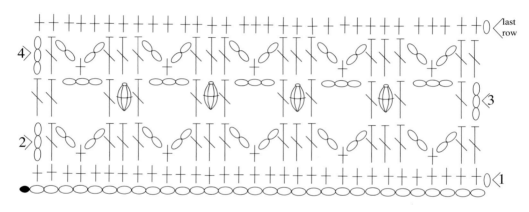

Foundation chain: With Col A make 32 ch.

Row 1: (right side) dc (US sc) in 2nd ch from hook and in each ch across—31 dc (US sc).

Row 2: 3 ch [count as tr (US dc) now and throughout, beginning chain], turn, tr (US dc) in next st, *2 ch, skip next st, dc (US sc) in next st, 2 ch, skip next st, tr (US dc) in each next 3 sts, repeat from * across ending with tr (US dc) in each last 2 sts—10 x 2-ch sps.

Row 3: 3 ch, turn, tr (US dc) in next st, *3 ch, tr (US dc) in next tr (US dc), in next st work PC, tr (US dc) in next st, repeat from * across ending with tr (US dc) in each last 2 sts, 4 x popcorns—5 x 3-ch sps.

Row 4: 3 ch, turn, tr (US dc) in next st, *2 ch, dc (US sc) in next 3-ch sp, 2 ch, tr (US dc) in each next 3 sts, repeat from * across ending with tr (US dc) in each last 2 sts—10 x 2-ch sps.

Subsequent rows: repeat rows 3 and 4 to desired size ending with row 4, then work last row as follows.

Last row: 1 ch, turn, dc (US sc) in each st and in each 2-ch sp across—do not finish off—work 2 rounds of edging in working colour before finishing off.

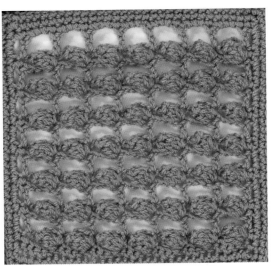 **Popcorn (PC):** Work 4 tr (US dc) in st indicated, drop loop from hook, insert hook in first st of group, hook dropped loop and draw through.

Square 10

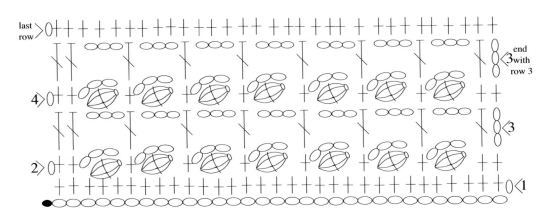

Foundation chain: With Col A make 32 ch.

Row 1: dc (US sc) in 2nd ch from hook and in each ch across—31 dc (US sc).

Row 2: (right side) 1 ch, turn, dc (US sc) in first 2 sts, *3 ch, work PC in same st, skip next 3 sts, dc (US sc) in next st, repeat from * across ending with dc (US sc) in last st—10 x dc (US sc) + 7 x popcorns.

Row 3: 3 ch [count as tr (US dc) now and throughout, beginning chain], tr (US dc) in next st, *3 ch, tr (US dc) in next dc (US sc), repeat from * across ending with tr (US dc) in last st—7 x 3-ch sps + 10 tr (US dc).

Row 4: 1 ch, turn, dc (US sc) in first 2 sts, *3 ch, work PC in same st, dc (US sc) in next tr (US dc), repeat from * across ending with dc (US sc) in last st.

Subsequent rows: repeat rows 3 and 4 to desired size ending with row 3, then work last row as follows.

Last row: 1 ch, turn, dc (US sc) in each st and 3 dc (US sc) in each 3-ch sp across—do not finish off—work 2 rounds of edging in working colour before finishing off.

Popcorn (PC): Work 4 tr (US dc) in st indicated, drop loop from hook, insert hook in first st of tr (US dc) group, hook dropped loop and draw through, 1 ch to close.

Square 11

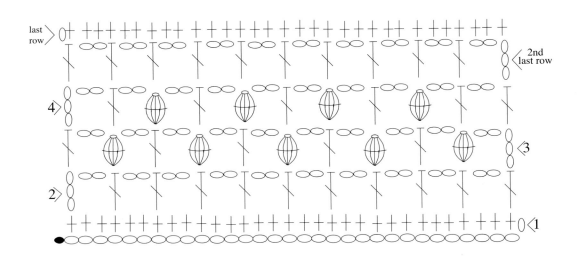

Foundation chain: With Col A make 32 ch.

Row 1: (right side) dc (US sc) in 2nd ch from hook and in each ch across—31 dc (US sc).

Row 2: 5 ch [count as tr (US dc) + 2-ch sp, now and throughout, beginning chain], turn, *skip next 2 sts, tr (US dc) in next st, 2 ch, repeat from * across—11 x tr (US dc) + 10 x 2-ch sps.

Row 3: 5 ch, *skip next 2-ch sp, work PC in next st, 2 ch, skip next 2-ch sp, tr (US dc) in next st, 2 ch, repeat from * across ending with tr (US dc) in 3rd ch of beginning chain—5 x popcorns + 6 x tr (US dc).

Row 4: 5 ch, *skip next 2-ch sp, tr (US dc) in next st, 2 ch, skip next 2-ch sp, in next st work [whfb] PC, 2 ch, repeat from * across ending with, tr (US dc) in 3rd ch of beginning chain—4 x popcorns + 7 x tr (US dc).

Subsequent rows: repeat rows 3 and 4 to desired size, then work 2 rows as follows.

2nd last row: 5 ch, turn, *skip 2 sts, tr (US dc) in next st, 2 ch, repeat from * across—11 x tr (US dc) + 10 x 2-ch sps.

Last row: 1 ch, turn, dc (US sc) in each st and 2 dc (US sc) in each 2-ch sp across to beginning chain, dc (US sc) in 3rd ch of beginning chain—do not finish off— work 2 last rounds of edging in working colour before finishing off.

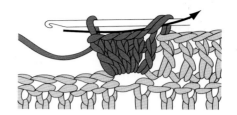

Popcorn (PC): Work 5 tr (US dc) in st indicated, drop loop from hook, * insert hook in first st of group, **pick up dropped loop and draw through, 1ch to close.

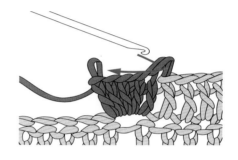

[whfb] = work hook from back: Work PC as above to *, insert hook in first st of group from the back then complete stitch from ** as above.

Square 12

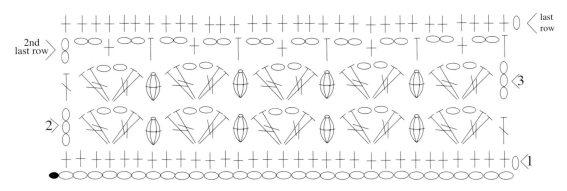

Foundation chain: With Col A make 32 ch.

Row 1: dc (US sc) in 2nd ch from hook and in each ch across—31 dc (US sc).

Row 2: (right side) 3 ch [count as tr (US dc) now and throughout, beginning chain], turn, *skip next 2 sts, in next st work [2tr (US dc), 2 ch, 2 tr (US dc)], skip next 2 sts, work PC in next st, repeat from * across ending with tr (US dc) in last st—5 x 2-ch sps + 4 x popcorns.

Row 3: 3 ch, turn, *work [2 tr (US dc), 2 ch, 2 tr (US dc)] in next 2-ch sp, skip next 2 sts, work [whfb] PC in next st, repeat from * across ending with tr (US dc) in top of beginning chain—5 x 2-ch sps + 4 x popcorns.

Subsequent rows: repeat rows 2 and 3 to desired size then work 2 last rows as follows.

2nd last row: 4 ch [count as htr (US hdc) + 2-ch sp], turn, *dc (US sc) in next 2-ch sp, 2 ch, skip next 2 sts, htr (US hdc) in next st, 2 ch, repeat from * across to beginning chain, htr (US hdc) in top of beginning chain.

Last row: 1 ch, turn, dc (US sc) in each st and 2 dc (US sc) in each 2-ch sp across to beginning chain, dc (US sc) in 2nd ch of beginning chain—do not finish off— work 2 rounds of edging in working colour before finishing off.

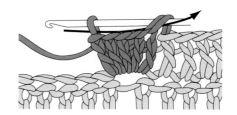

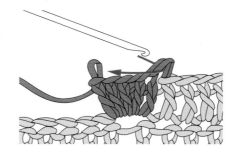

Popcorn (PC): Work 4 tr (US dc) in st indicated, drop loop from hook, *insert hook in first st of group, **pick up dropped loop and draw through, 1ch to close.

[whfb] = work hook from back: Work PC as above to *, insert hook in first st of group from the back then complete stitch from ** as above.

Square 13

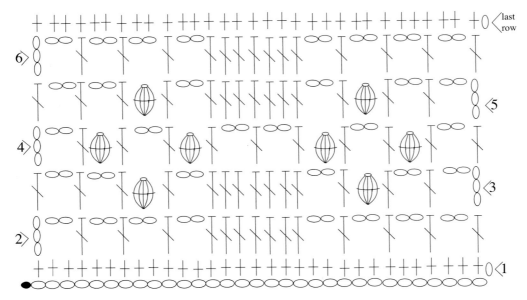

Foundation chain: With Col A make 32 ch.

Row 1: (right side) dc (US sc) in 2nd ch from hook and in each ch across—31 dc (US sc).

Row 2: 5 ch [count as tr (US dc) + 2-ch sp, now and throughout, beginning chain], turn, skip next 2 sts, [tr (US dc) in next st, 2 ch, skip next 2 sts] 3 times, tr (US dc) in next 7 sts, [2 ch, skip next 2 sts, tr (US dc) in next st] 4 times—15 x tr (US dc) + 8 x 2-ch sps.

Row 3: 5 ch, turn, tr (US dc) in next tr (US dc), 2 ch, tr (US dc) in next tr (US dc), work PC in next 2-ch sp, tr (US dc) in next tr (US dc), 2 ch, tr (US dc) in next 7 sts, 2 ch, tr (US dc) in next tr (US dc), work PC in next 2-ch sp, then work [tr (US dc) in next st, 2 ch] twice, ending with tr (US dc) in 3rd ch of beginning chain—15 x tr (US dc) + 6 x 2-ch sps + 2 x popcorns.

Row 4: 5 ch, turn, *tr (US dc) in next tr (US dc), work [whfb] PC in next 2-ch sp, tr (US dc) in next tr (US dc), 2 ch, tr (US dc) in next tr (US dc), work [whfb] PC in next 2-ch sp**, then work [tr (US dc) in next st, 2 ch, skip next 2 sts] twice, repeat from * to ** once more, ending with tr (US dc) in next tr (US dc), 2 ch, tr (US dc) in 3rd ch of beginning chain.

Row 5: 5 ch, turn, tr (US dc) in next tr (US dc), 2 ch, tr (US dc) in next tr (US dc), work PC in next 2-ch sp, tr (US dc) in next tr (US dc), 2 ch, tr (US dc) in next tr (US dc), then work [2 tr (US dc) in next 2-ch sp, tr (US dc) in next tr (US dc)] twice, 2 ch, tr (US dc) in next tr (US dc), work PC in next 2-ch sp, then work [tr (US dc) in next st, 2 ch] twice, ending with last tr (US dc) in 3rd ch of beginning chain—15 x tr (US dc) + 6 x 2-ch sps + 2 x popcorns.

Row 6: 5 ch, turn, [tr (US dc) in next tr (US dc), 2 ch] 3 times, tr (US dc) in next 7 sts, then work [2 ch, tr (US dc) in next st] 4 times, ending with last tr (US dc) in 3rd ch of beginning chain, 15 x tr (US dc)—8 x 2-ch sps.

Subsequent rows: repeat rows 3 to 6 to desired size ending with row 6, then work last row as follows.

Last row: 1 ch, turn, dc (US sc) in each st and 2 dc (US sc) in each 2-ch sp across to beginning chain, dc (US sc) in 3rd ch of beginning chain—do not finish off—work 2 rounds of edging in working colour before finishing off.

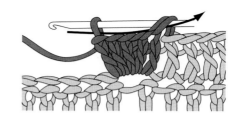

Popcorn (PC): Work 5 tr (US dc) in st indicated, drop loop from hook, *insert hook in first st of group, **pick up dropped loop and draw through, 1 ch to close.

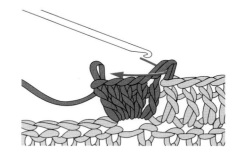

[whfb] = work hook from back: Work PC as above to, *insert hook in first st of group from the back, then complete stitch from ** as above.

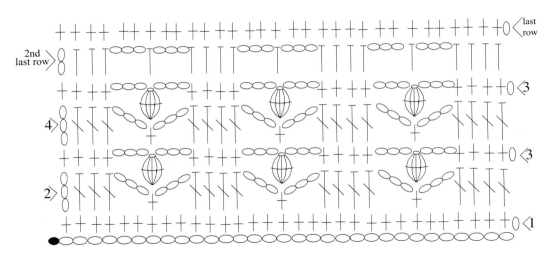

Foundation chain: With Col A make 32 ch.

Row 1: (right side) dc (US sc) in 2nd ch from hook and in each ch across—31 dc (US sc).

Row 2: 3 ch [count as tr (US dc) now and throughout, beginning chain], turn, tr (US dc) in next 3 sts, *3 ch, skip next 2 sts, dc (US sc) in next st, 3 ch, skip next 2 sts, tr (US dc) in next 4 sts, repeat from * across—6 x 3-ch sps + 12 x tr (US dc).

Row 3: 1 ch, turn, dc (US sc) in first 4 sts, *3 ch, PC in next dc (US sc), 3 ch, dc (US sc) in next 4 sts, repeat from * across—6 x 3-ch sps + 12 x dc (US sc).

Row 4: 3 ch, turn, tr (US dc) in next 3 sts, *3 ch, dc (US sc) in next PC, 3 ch, tr (US dc) in next 4 sts, repeat from * across—6 x 3-ch sps + 12 x tr (US dc).

Subsequent rows: repeat rows 3 and 4 to desired size ending with row 3, then work 2 last rows as follows.

2nd last row: 2 ch [counts as htr (US hdc)], turn, htr (US hdc) in next 3 sts, *3 ch, htr (US hdc) in next PC, 3 ch, htr (US hdc) in next 4 sts, repeat from * across—6 x 3-ch sps.

Last row: 1 ch, turn, dc (US sc) in each st and 2 dc (US sc) in each 3-ch sp across—do not finish off—work 2 rounds of edging in working colour before finishing off.

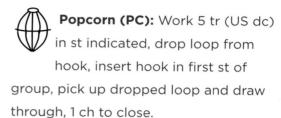 **Popcorn (PC):** Work 5 tr (US dc) in st indicated, drop loop from hook, insert hook in first st of group, pick up dropped loop and draw through, 1 ch to close.

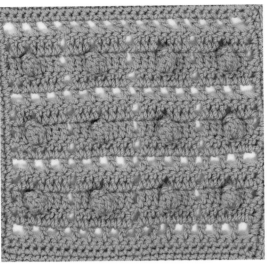

Square 15

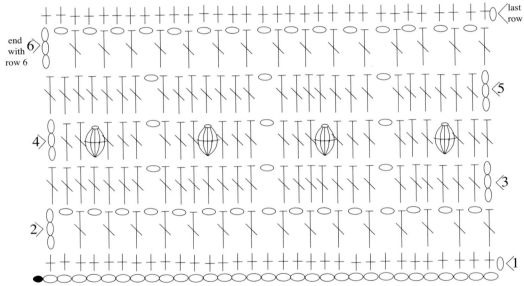

Foundation chain: With Col A make 32 ch.

Row 1: dc (US sc) in 2nd ch from hook and in each ch across—31 dc (US sc).

Row 2: (right side) 4 ch [count as tr (US dc) + 1-ch sp, now and throughout, beginning chain], turn, *skip next st, tr (US dc) in next st, 1 ch, repeat from * across—15 x 1-ch sps + 16 x tr (US dc).

Row 3: 3 ch [count as tr (US dc), now and throughout, beginning chain], turn, [tr (US dc) in next 1-ch sp and in next st] 3 times, *1 ch, skip next 1-ch sp, tr (US dc) in next st, [tr (US dc) in next 1-ch sp and in next st] 3 times, repeat from * across—3 x 1-ch sps + 28 x tr (US dc).

Row 4: 3 ch, turn, tr (US dc) in next 2 sts, *work PC in next st, tr (US dc) in each next 3 sts, 1 ch, skip next 1-ch sp, tr (US dc) in each next 3 sts, repeat from * across—3 x 1-ch sp + 24 x tr (US dc) + 4 x popcorns.

Row 5: 3 ch, tr (US dc) in next 6 sts, *1 ch, skip next 1-ch sp, tr (US dc) in next 7 sts, repeat from * across—3 x 1-ch sps + 28 x tr (US dc).

Row 6: 4 ch, turn, *skip next st, tr (US dc) in next st, repeat from * across—15 x 1-ch sps + 16 x tr (US dc).

Subsequent rows: repeat rows 3 to 6 to desired size ending with row 6, then work last row as follows.

Last row: 1 ch, turn, dc (US sc) in each st and in each 1-ch sp across—do not finish off—work 2 rounds of edging in working colour before finishing off.

Popcorn (PC): Work 5 tr (US dc) in st indicated, drop loop from hook, insert hook in first st of group, pick up dropped loop and draw through, 1 ch to close.

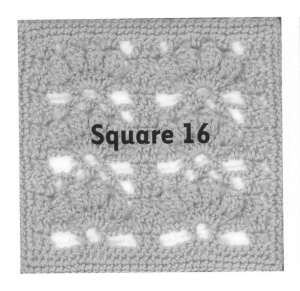

Foundation chain: With Col A make 32 ch.

Row 1: dc (US sc) in 2nd ch from hook and in each ch across—31 dc (US sc).

Row 2: (right side) 3 ch [count as tr (US dc) now and throughout, beginning chain], turn, tr (US dc) in next 2 sts, *5 ch, skip 4 next sts, dc (US sc) in next st, 3 ch, skip next st, dc (US sc) in next st, 5 ch, skip next 4 sts, tr (US dc) in next 3 sts, repeat from * across—4 x 5-ch sps + 9 x tr (US dc) + 2 x 3-ch sps.

Row 3: 3 ch, turn, tr (US dc) in next 2 sts, *2 ch, [dc (US sc), 1 ch] in next 5-ch sp, 7 tr (US dc) in next 3-ch sp, [1 ch, dc (US sc)] in next 5-ch sp, 2 ch, tr (US dc) in each next 3 tr (US dc), repeat from * across—4 x 2-ch sps + 23 x tr (US dc) + 4 x dc (US sc).

Row 4: 3 ch, turn, tr (US dc) in next 2 sts, *1 ch, PC in next tr (US dc), (4 ch, skip next st, PC in next st) 3 times, 1 ch, tr (US dc) in each next 3 tr (US dc), repeat from * across—9 x tr (US dc) + 8 x popcorns + 6 x 4-ch sps.

Row 5: 3 ch, turn, tr (US dc) in next 2 sts, *2 ch, dc (US sc) in next 4-ch sp, [3 ch, dc (US sc) in next 4-ch sp] twice, 2 ch, tr (US dc) in each next 3 tr (US dc), repeat from * across—9 x tr (US dc) + 4 x 2-ch sps + 4 x 3-ch sps.

Row 6: 3 ch, turn, tr (US dc) in next 2 sts, *5 ch, dc (US sc) in next 3-ch sp, 3 ch, dc (US sc) in next 3-ch sp, 5 ch, tr (US dc) in next 3 tr (US dc), repeat from * across—9 x tr (US dc) + 4 x dc (US sc) + 4 x 5-ch sps + 2 x 3-ch sps.

Subsequent rows: repeat rows 3 to 6 to desired size ending with row 5, then work 1 last row as follows.

Last row: 1 ch, turn, dc (US sc) in each st, 2 dc (US sc) in each 2-ch sp and 3-ch sp across—do not finish off—work 2 rounds of edging in working colour before finishing off.

Popcorn (PC): Work 5 tr (US dc) in st indicated, drop loop from hook, insert hook in first st of tr (US dc) group, pick up dropped loop and draw through, 1 ch to close.

Square 17

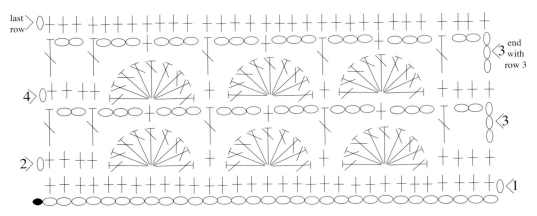

Foundation chain: With Col A make 32 ch.

Row 1: dc (US sc) in 2nd ch from hook and in each ch across—31 dc (US sc).

Row 2: (right side) 1 ch, turn, dc (US sc) in first 4 sts, *skip next 3 sts, work 9 Ltr (US Ldc) in next st (fan made), skip next 3 sts, dc (US sc) in next st, repeat from * across ending with dc (US sc) in each last 4 sts—3 x fans.

Row 3: 5 ch [count as tr (US dc) + 2 ch, now and throughout, beginning chain], skip 2 sts, tr (US dc) in next st, *3 ch, dc (US sc) in 5th st of next fan, 3 ch, tr (US dc) in next dc (US sc), repeat from * across ending with 2 ch, skip 2 sts, tr (US dc) in last st—6 x 3-ch sps + 2 x 2-ch sps.

Row 4: 1 ch, turn, dc (US sc) in first st, 2 dc (US sc) in next 2-ch sp, dc (US sc) in next st, *work 9 Ltr (US Ldc) in next dc (US sc), dc (US sc) in next tr (US dc), repeat from * across ending with 2 dc (US sc) in 2-ch sp and dc (US sc) in 3rd ch of beginning chain—3 x fans.

Subsequent rows: repeat rows 3 and 4 to desired size ending with row 3, then work last row as follows.

Last row: 1 ch, turn, dc (US sc) in each st, 2 dc (US sc) in each 2-ch sp and 3 dc (US sc) in each 3-ch sp across—do not finish off—work 2 rounds of edging in working colour before finishing off.

Long treble/Ltr (US long double crochet/Ldc): YO, insert hook into stitch indicated and draw up a long loop (approx 1.5 cm / ½ in), (YO and draw through 2 loops) twice.

Foundation chain: With Col A make 32 ch.

Row 1: (right side) dc (US sc) in 2nd ch from hook and in each ch across—31 dc (US sc).

Row 2: 5 ch [count as tr (US dc) + 2-ch sp, now and throughout, beginning chain], turn, tr (US dc) in same st, *3 ch, skip next 3 sts, dc (US sc) in next 3 sts, 3 ch, skip next 3 sts, in next st work [tr (US dc), 3 ch, tr (US dc)] (V-st made), repeat from * across ending with skip next 3 sts, [tr (US dc), 2ch, tr (US dc)] in last st—4 x V-st + 8 x 3-ch-sps + 2 x 2-ch-sps + 9 x dc (US sc).

Row 3: 3 ch [count as tr (US dc), now and throughout, beginning chain], 3 tr (US dc) in 2-ch sp, *3 ch, dc (US sc) in 2nd st of next dc (US sc) group, 3 ch, work 7 tr (US dc) in 3-ch sp of next V-st, repeat from * across ending with 3 tr (US dc) in 2-ch sp and tr (US dc) in 3rd ch of beginning chain—2 x 4-tr (US dc) fans + 2 x 7-tr (US dc) fans.

Row 4: 1 ch, turn, dc (US sc) in first 4 sts, *5 ch, skip next 3-ch sp, dc (US sc) and 3-ch sp, dc (US sc) in each next 7 sts, repeat from * across ending with dc (US sc) in each last 4 sts—3 x 5-ch sps + 22 x dc (US sc).

Row 5: 1 ch, turn, dc (US sc) in first 2 sts, *3 ch, work V-st in 3rd ch of next 5-ch sp, 3 ch, skip next 2 dc (US sc), dc (US sc) in next 3 sts, repeat from * across to last 4 sts, skip 2 sts, dc (US sc) in last 2 sts—3 x V-st + 9 x 3-ch-sps + 10 x dc (US sc).

Row 6: 1 ch, turn, dc (US sc) in first st, *3 ch, work 7 tr (US dc) in 3-ch sp of next V-st, 3 ch, dc (US sc) in 2nd st of next dc (US sc) group, repeat from * across ending with dc (US sc) in last st—3 x 7-tr (US dc) fans.

Row 7: 1 ch, turn, dc (US sc) in first st, 2 ch, *dc (US sc) in each next 7 sts, 5 ch, skip next 3-ch sp, dc (US sc) and 3-ch sp, repeat from * across ending with 2 ch and dc (US sc) in last st—2 x 5-ch sps + 2 x 2-ch sps.

Row 8: 5 ch, turn, tr (US dc) in same st, *3 ch, skip 2 sts, dc (US sc) in next 3 sts, 3 ch, work V-st in 3rd ch of next 5-ch sp, repeat from * across ending with 3 ch, [tr (US dc), 2 ch, tr (US dc)] in last st—4 x V-st + 8 x 3-ch-sps + 2 x 2-ch-sps + 9 x dc (US sc).

Subsequent rows: repeat rows 3 to 8 to desired size ending with row 4, then work 2 last rows as follows.

2nd last row: 3 ch, turn, tr (US dc) in same st, *3 ch, tr (US dc) in 3rd ch of next 5-ch sp, 3 ch, skip 2 dc (US sc), dc (US sc) in next 3 sts, repeat from * across ending with 2 tr (US dc) in last st—10 x 2-ch sps.

Last row: 1 ch, turn, dc (US sc) in each st and 3 dc (US sc) in each 3-ch sp across—do not finish off—work 2 rounds of edging in working colour before finishing off.

Square 19

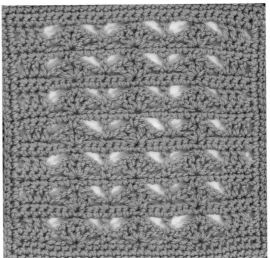

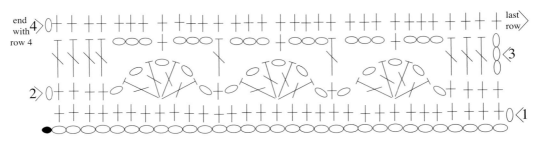

Foundation chain: With Col A make 32 ch.

Row 1: (right side) dc (US sc) in 2nd ch from hook and in each ch across—31 dc (US sc).

Row 2: 1 ch, turn, dc (US sc) in first 4 sts, 1 ch, *skip next 3 sts, in next st work [tr (US dc), 1 ch] 4 times (fan made), skip next 3 sts, [dc (US sc), 1 ch] in next st, repeat from * across to last 4 sts, dc (US sc) in each last 4 sts—3 x fans + 8 x tr (US dc).

Row 3: 3 ch [count as tr (US dc) now and throughout, beginning chain], turn, tr (US dc) in next 3 sts, *3 ch, dc (US sc) in 2nd 1-ch sp of next fan, 3 ch, tr (US dc) in next dc (US sc), repeat from * across ending with tr (US dc) in each last 4 sts—10 x tr (US dc) + 6 x 3-ch sps.

Row 4: 1 ch, turn, dc (US sc) in each st and 3 dc (US sc) in each 3-ch sp across to beginning chain, dc (US sc) in top of beginning chain—31 dc (US sc).

Subsequent rows: repeat rows 2 to 4 to desired size ending with row 4—do not finish off—work 2 rounds of edging in working colour before finishing off.

Square 20

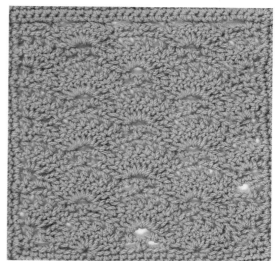

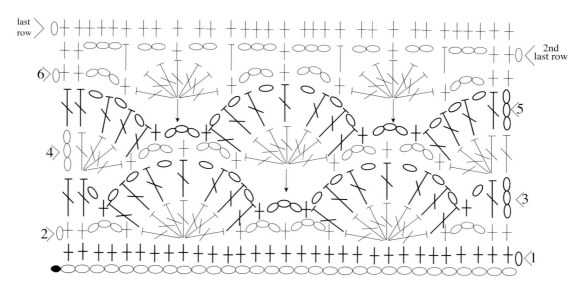

Foundation chain: With Col A make 32 ch.

Row 1: dc (US sc) in 2nd ch from hook and in each ch across—31 dc (US sc).

Row 2: (right side) 1 ch, turn, dc (US sc) in first 2 sts, 3 ch, skip next 2 sts, dc (US sc) in next st, *skip next 3 sts, work 7 tr (US dc) in next st, skip next 3 sts, dc (US sc) in next st**, work [3 ch, skip 2 sts, dc (US sc) in next st] twice, repeat from * to ** once more, ending with 3 ch, skip 2 sts, dc (US sc) in each last 2 sts—2 x 7-tr (US dc) fans + 4 x 3-ch sps.

Row 3: 3 ch [count as tr (US dc) now and throughout, beginning chain], turn, tr (US dc) in next st, 1 ch, *dc (US sc) in next 3-ch sp, work [tr (US dc) in next tr (US dc), 1 ch] 6 times, tr (US dc) in next tr (US dc) **, dc (US sc) in next 3-ch sp, 3 ch, repeat from * to ** once more, ending with dc (US sc) in last 3-ch sp, 1 ch, tr (US dc) in each last 2 sts—2 x extended 7-tr (US dc) fans + 1 x 3-ch sp.

Row 4: 3 ch, 4 tr (US dc) in next st, skip next two 1-ch sps, *dc (US sc) in next 1-ch sp, 3 ch, skip next [tr (US dc) and 1-ch sp], dc (US sc) in next st, 3 ch, skip next [1-ch sp and tr (US dc)], dc (US sc) in next 1-ch sp**, work 7 tr (US dc) in next 3-ch sp, skip next 1-ch sp, repeat from * to ** once more, ending with skip two 1-ch sps, 4 tr (US dc) in next st and tr (US dc) in top of beginning chain—1 x 7-tr (US dc) fan + 2 x 4-tr (US dc) fans.

Row 5: 3 ch, turn, [tr (US dc) in next st, 1 ch] 3 times, tr (US dc) in next st, *dc (US sc) in next 3-ch sp, 3 ch, dc (US sc) in next 3-ch sp**, tr (US dc) in next tr (US dc), [1 ch, tr (US dc) in next tr (US dc)] 6 times, repeat from * to ** once more, ending with [tr (US dc) in next st, 1 ch] 3 times and tr (US dc) in each last 2 sts.

Row 6: 1 ch, turn, dc (US sc) in first 2 sts, 3 ch, skip next [1-ch sp and tr (US dc)], dc (US sc) in next 1-ch sp, 7 tr (US dc) in next 3-ch sp, skip next [1-ch sp

and tr (US dc)], dc (US sc) in next 1-ch sp, 3 ch, skip next [tr (US dc) and 1-ch sp) dc (US sc) in next st, 3 ch, skip next [1-ch sp and tr (US dc)], dc (US sc) in next 1-ch sp, 7 tr (US dc) in next 3-ch sp, skip next [1-ch sp and tr (US dc)], dc (US sc) in next 1-ch sp, 3 ch, skip next [tr (US dc) and 1-ch sp], dc (US sc) in each last 2 sts—2 x 7-tr (US dc) fans + 4 x 3-ch sps.

Subsequent rows: repeat rows 3 to 6 to desired size ending with row 6, then work 2 last rows as follows.

2nd last row: 1 ch, turn, dc (US sc) in next first 2 sts, 3 ch, htr (US hdc) in next dc (US sc), 2 ch, dc (US sc) in 4th st of next fan, 2 ch, htr (US hdc) in next dc (US sc), 3 ch, dc (US sc) in next dc (US sc), 3 ch, htr (US hdc) in next dc (US sc), 2 ch, dc (US sc) in 4th st of next fan, 2 ch htr (US hdc) in next dc (US sc), 3 ch, dc (US sc) in each last 2 sts.

Last row: 1 ch, turn, dc (US sc) in each st, 2 dc (US sc) in each 2-ch sp and 3 dc (US sc) in each 3-ch sp across—do not finish off—work 2 rounds of edging in working colour before finishing off.

Square 21

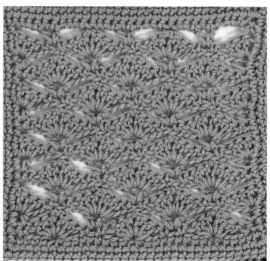

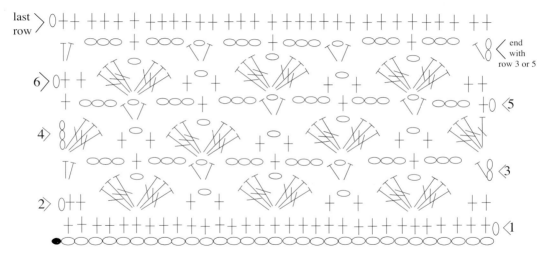

Foundation chain: With Col A make 32 ch.

Row 1: (right side) dc (US sc) in 2nd ch from hook and in each ch across—31 dc (US sc).

Row 2: 1 ch, turn, dc (US sc) in first 2 sts, *skip next 3 sts, in next st work [3tr (US dc), 1 ch, 3 tr (US dc)], skip next 3 sts, dc (US sc) in next st, 1 ch, skip next st, dc (US sc) in next st, repeat from *

across to last 2 sts, dc (US sc) in last 2 sts—5 x 1-ch sps.

Row 3: 2 ch [count as htr (US hdc) now and throughout, beginning chain], turn, htr (US hdc) in same st, *3 ch, dc (US sc) in next 1-ch sp, 3 ch, work [htr (US hdc), 1 ch, htr (US hdc)] in next 1-ch sp, repeat from * across, ending with 3 ch and 2 htr (US hdc) in last st—6 x 3-ch sps + 2 x 1-ch sps.

Row 4: 3 ch, turn, 3 tr (US dc) in same st, *skip next st and next 2 ch, dc (US sc) in next ch, 1 ch, skip next st, dc (US sc) in next ch, work [3tr (US dc), 1 ch, 3 tr (US dc)] in next 1-ch sp, repeat from * across to beginning chain, 4 tr (US dc) in top of beginning chain—5 x 1-ch sps.

Row 5: 1 ch, turn, dc (US sc) in first st, *3 ch, work [htr (US hdc), 1 ch, htr (US hdc)] in next 1-ch sp, 3 ch, dc (US sc) in next 1-ch sp, repeat from * across ending with 3 ch and dc (US sc) in top of beginning chain.

Row 6: 1 ch, turn, dc (US sc) in first st and next ch, *skip 2 ch, in next 1-ch sp work [3 tr (US dc), 1 ch, 3 tr (US dc)], skip 2 ch, dc (US sc) in next ch, 1 ch, skip next st, dc (US sc) in next ch, repeat from * across ending with skip 2 ch, dc (US sc) in next ch and dc (US sc) in last st—5 x 1-ch sps.

Subsequent rows: repeat rows 3 to 6 to desired size ending with row 3 or row 5, then work last row as follows.

Last row: 1 ch, turn, dc (US sc) in each st and in each 1-ch sp and 3 dc (US sc) in each 3-ch sp across—do not finish off—work 2 rounds of edging in working colour before finishing off.

Square 22

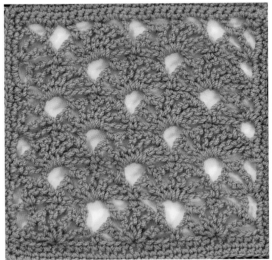

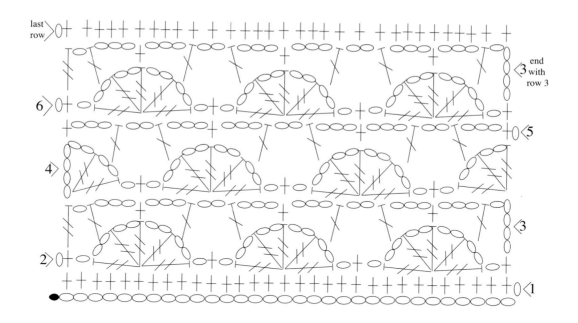

Foundation chain: With Col A make 32 ch.

Row 1: (right side) dc (US sc) in 2nd ch from hook and in each ch across—31 dc (US sc).

Row 2: 1 ch, turn, dc (US sc) in first st, *1 ch, skip next 4 sts, in next st work [dtr (US tr), 2 ch) 4 times and dtr (US tr), 1 ch], skip next 4 sts, dc (US sc) in next st, repeat from * across—3 x fans.

Row 3: 5 ch [count as dtr (US tr) + 1 ch, now and throughout, beginning chain], turn, *tr (US dc) in next 2-ch sp, 3 ch, skip next st and 2-ch sp, dc (US sc) in next st, 3 ch, skip next 2-ch sp and next st, tr (US dc) in next 2-ch sp, 2 ch, repeat from * across ending with 1 ch

and dtr (US tr) in last st—6 x 3-ch sps + 2 x 2-ch sps.

Row 4: 6 ch [count as dtr (US tr) + 2 ch, now and throughout, beginning chain], in first st work [dtr (US tr), 2 ch, dtr (US tr), 1 ch], *dc (US sc) in next dc (US sc), 1 ch, in next 2-ch sp work [{dtr (US tr), 2 ch} 4 times and dtr (US tr), 1 ch], repeat from * across ending with [dtr (US tr), 2 ch, dtr (US tr), 2 ch, dtr (US tr)] in 4th ch of beginning ch—2 x fans.

Row 5: 1 ch, turn, dc (US sc) in first st, *3 ch, skip next 2-ch sp and tr (US dc), tr (US dc) in next 2-ch sp, 2 ch, tr (US dc) in next 2-ch sp, 3 ch, skip next tr (US dc) and 2-ch sp, dc (US sc) in next st, repeat from * across to beginning chain, dc (US sc) in 4th ch of beginning chain—6 x 3-ch sps + 2 x 2-ch sps.

Row 6: 1 ch, turn, dc (US sc) in first st, *1 ch, in next 2-ch sp work [(dtr (US tr), 2 ch) 4 times and dtr (US tr), 1 ch], dc (US sc) in next dc (US sc), repeat from * across—3 x fans.

Subsequent rows: repeat rows 3 to 6 to desired size ending with row 5, then work last row as follows.

Last row: 1 ch, turn, dc (US sc) in each st, 3 dc (US sc) in each 3-ch sp and 1 dc (US sc) in each 2-ch sp across (leaving 1-ch sps unused)—do not finish off— work 2 rounds of edging in working colour before finishing off.

Double treble/dtr (US treble/tr): YO twice, insert hook in st or sp indicated and draw up a loop, YO and draw through 2 loops on hook 3 times.

COLOUR GROUP B

Square 23

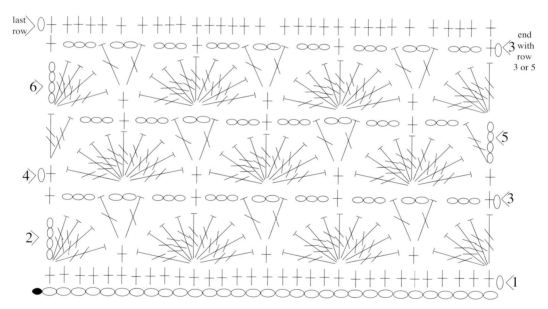

Foundation chain: With Col B make 32 ch.

Row 1: dc (US sc) in 2nd ch from hook and in each ch across—31 dc (US sc).

Row 2: (right side) 4 ch [count as dtr (US tr) now and throughout, beginning chain], turn, 4 dtr (US tr) in same st, *skip next 4 sts, dc (US sc) in next st, skip next 4 sts, 9 dtr (US tr) in next st (fan made), repeat from * across ending with 5 dtr (US tr) in last st—2 x 9-dtr (US tr) fans + 2 x 5-dtr (US tr) fans.

Row 3: 1 ch, turn, dc (US sc) in first st, *3 ch, in next dc (US sc) work [tr (US dc), 2ch, tr (US dc)], 3 ch, dc (US sc) in 5th st of next fan, repeat from * across to beginning chain, dc (US sc) in top of beginning chain—6 x 3-ch sps + 3 x 2-ch sps.

Row 4: 1 ch, turn, dc (US sc) in first st, *9 dtr (US tr) in next 2-ch sp, dc (US sc) in next dc (US sc), repeat from * across—3 x fans.

Row 5: 4 ch, turn, dtr (US tr) in same st, *3 ch, dc (US sc) in 5th st of next fan, 3 ch, in next dc (US sc) work [tr (US dc), 2 ch, tr (US dc)], repeat from * across ending with 2 dtr (US tr) in last st—6 x 3-ch sps + 2 x 2-ch sps.

Row 6: 4 ch, turn, 4 dtr (US tr) in same st, *dc (US sc) in next dc (US sc), 9 dtr (US tr) in next 2-ch sp, repeat from * across ending with 5 dtr (US tr) in top of beginning chain—2 x 9-dtr (US tr) fans + 2 x 5-dtr (US tr) fans.

Subsequent rows: repeat rows 3 to 6 to desired size ending with row 3 or 5, then work last row as follows.

Last row: 1 ch, turn, dc (US sc) in each st, 1 dc (US sc) in each 2-ch sp and 3 dc (US sc) in each 3-ch sp across—do not finish off—work 2 rounds of edging in working colour before finishing off.

Double treble/dtr (US treble/tr): YO twice, insert hook in st or sp and draw up a loop, YO and draw through 2 loops on hook 3 times.

Square 24

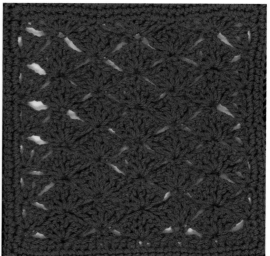

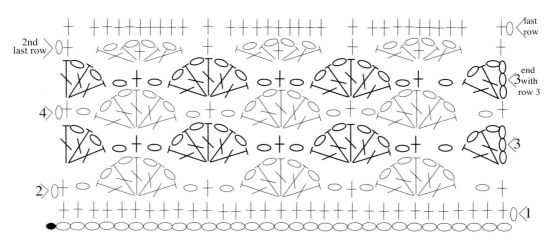

Foundation chain: With Col B make 32 ch.

Row 1: (right side) dc (US sc) in 2nd ch from hook and in each ch across—31 dc (US sc).

Row 2: 1 ch, turn, dc (US sc) in first st, 1 ch, *skip next 4 sts, in next st work [tr (US dc), 1 ch] 5 times (fan made), skip next 4 sts, dc (US sc) in next st, 1 ch, repeat from * across—3 x fans.

Row 3: 4 ch, [count as tr (US dc) + 1 ch, now and throughout, beginning chain], turn, in same st work [tr (US dc), 1 ch] twice, *dc (US sc) in 3rd st of next fan, 1 ch, in next dc (US sc) work [tr (US dc), 1 ch] 5 times, repeat from * across ending with [1 ch, tr (US dc), 1 ch, tr (US dc), 1 ch, tr (US dc)] in last st—2 x fans.

Row 4: 1 ch, turn, dc (US sc) in first st, 1 ch, *in next dc (US sc) work [tr (US dc), 1 ch] 5 times, dc (US sc) in 3rd st of next fan, 1 ch, repeat from * across ending with dc (US sc) in 3rd ch of beginning chain—3 x fans.

Subsequent rows: repeat rows 3 and 4 to desired size ending with row 3, then work 2 last rows as follows

2nd last row: 1 ch, turn, dc (US sc) in next first st, *in next dc (US sc) work [tr (US dc), 1 ch, htr (US hdc), 1 ch, dc (US sc), 1 ch, htr (US hdc), 1 ch, tr (US dc)], dc (US sc) in 3rd st of next fan, repeat from * across ending with dc (US sc) in 3rd ch of beginning chain—3 x shortened fans.

Last row: 1 ch, turn, dc (US sc) in each st and in each 1-ch sp across—do not finish off—work 2 rounds of edging in working colour before finishing off.

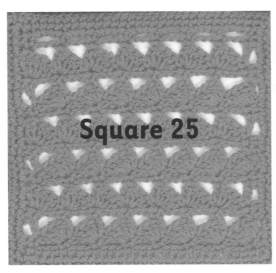

Square 25

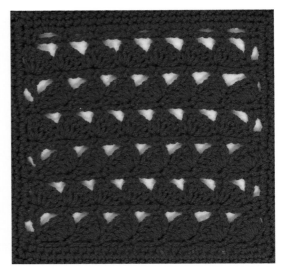

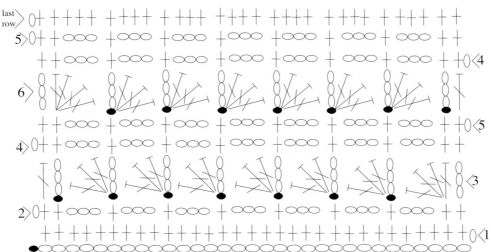

Foundation chain: With Col B make 32 ch.

Row 1: (right side) dc (US sc) in 2nd ch from hook and in each ch across—31 dc (US sc).

Row 2: 1 ch, turn, dc (US sc) in first 2 sts, *3 ch, skip next 3 sts, dc (US sc) in next st, repeat from * across ending with dc (US sc) in each last 2 sts—7 x 3-ch sps.

Row 3: 3 ch [count as tr (US dc) now and throughout, beginning chain], turn, 4 tr (US dc) in next st, *in next dc (US sc) work [ss, 3 ch, 3 tr (US dc)], repeat from * across to last 2 sts ending with (ss, 3 ch) [count as tr (US dc)] in next st and tr (US dc) in last st—7 x shells.

Row 4: 1 ch, turn, dc (US sc) in first 2 sts, *3 ch, dc (US sc) in top of next 3-ch of previous row, repeat from * across ending with dc (US sc) in each last 2 sts—7 x 3-ch sps.

Row 5: 1 ch, turn, dc (US sc) in first 2 sts, *3 ch, dc (US sc) in next dc (US sc), repeat from * across ending with dc (US sc) in each last 2 sts—7 x 3-ch sps.

Row 6: 3 ch, turn, 4 tr (US dc) in next st, in next dc (US sc) work [ss, 3 ch, 3 tr (US dc)], repeat from * across ending with (ss, 3 ch) [count as tr (US dc)] in next st and tr (US dc) in last st—7 x shells.

Row 7: repeat row 4.

Row 8: repeat row 5.

Subsequent rows: repeat rows 3 to 8 to desired size ending with row 5, then work last row as follows.

Last row: 1 ch, turn, dc (US sc) in each st and 3 dc (US sc) in each 3-ch sp across—do not finish off—work 2 rounds of edging in working colour before finishing off.

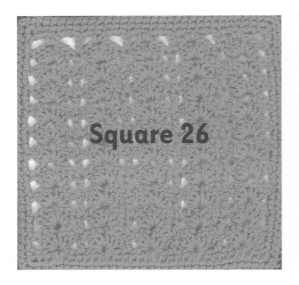

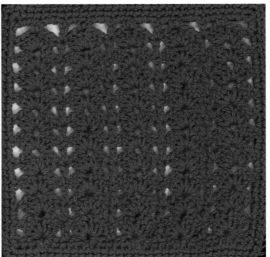

Square 26

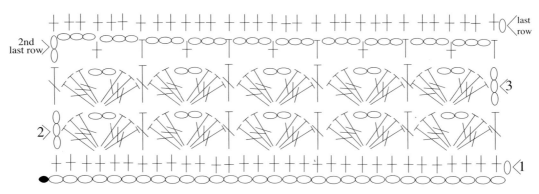

Foundation chain: With Col B make 32 ch.

Row 1: (right side) dc (US sc) in 2nd ch from hook and in each ch across—31 dc (US sc).

Row 2: 3 ch [count as tr (US dc) now and throughout, beginning chain], turn, *skip next 2 sts, in next st work [3 tr (US dc), 2 ch, 3 tr (US dc)], skip next 2 sts, tr (US dc) in next st, repeat from * across—10 x shells + 5 x 2-ch sps.

Row 3: 3 ch, turn, *in next 2-ch sp work [3 tr (US dc), 2 ch, 3 tr (US dc)], skip 3 next sts, tr (US dc) in next st, repeat from * across ending with tr (US dc) in 3rd ch of beginning chain—10 x shells + 5 x 2-ch sps.

Subsequent rows: repeat row 3 to desired size, then work 2 last rows as follows.

2nd last row: 5 ch [count as htr (US hdc) + 3 ch, now and throughout, beginning chain], turn, *dc (US sc) in next 2-ch sp, 3 ch, skip next 3 sts, htr (US hdc) in next st, 3 ch, repeat from * across ending with htr (US hdc) in 3rd ch of beginning chain—10 x 3-ch sps + 6 x htr (US hdc) + 5 x dc (US sc).

Last row: 1 ch, turn, dc (US sc) in each st and 2 dc (US sc) in each 3-ch sp across—do not finish off—work 2 rounds of edging in working colour before finishing off.

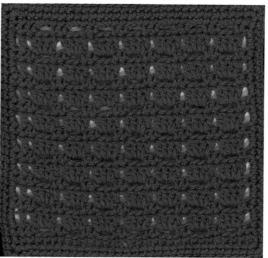

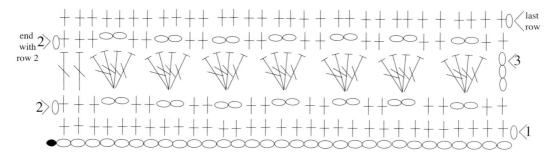

Foundation chain: With Col B make 32 ch.

Row 1: (right side) dc (US sc) in 2nd ch from hook and in each ch across—31 dc (US sc).

Row 2: 1 ch, turn, dc (US sc) in first 3 sts, *2 ch, skip next 2 sts, dc (US sc) in each next 2 sts, repeat from * across—7 x 2-ch sps.

Row 3: 3 ch [count as tr (US dc) now and throughout, beginning chain], turn, *work 4 tr (US dc) in next 2-ch sp, repeat from * across ending with tr (US dc) in each last 2 sts—7 x shells.

Subsequent rows: repeat rows 2 and 3 to desired size ending with row 2, then work last row as follows.

Last row: 1 ch, turn, dc (US sc) in each st and 2 dc (US sc) in each 2-ch sp across—do not finish off—work 2 rounds of edging in working colour before finishing off.

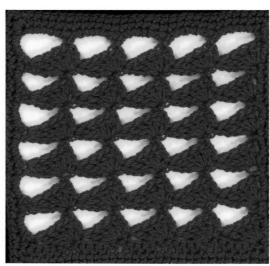

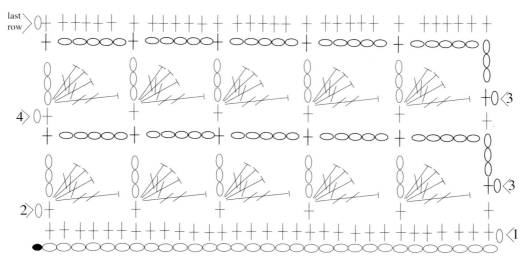

Foundation chain: With Col B make 32 ch.

Row 1: dc (US sc) in 2nd ch from hook and in each ch across—31 dc (US sc).

Row 2: (right side) 1 ch, turn, dc (US sc) in first st, *3 ch [count as tr (US dc), now and throughout], in same st work [3tr (US dc), 1 dtr (US tr)], skip next 5 sts, dc (US sc) in next st, repeat from * across—5 x shells.

Row 3: 1 ch, turn, dc (US sc) in first st, 8 ch [count as tr (US dc) + 5 ch, now and throughout, beginning chain], turn, *skip next 4 sts, dc (US sc) in top of next 3 ch of previous row, 5 ch, repeat from * across—5 x shells.

Row 4: 1 ch, turn, dc (US sc) in first st, *in same st work [3 ch, 3tr (US dc), 1 dtr (US tr)], skip next 5 ch, dc (US sc) in next st, repeat from * across to beginning chain, dc (US sc) in 3rd ch of beginning chain—5 x shells.

Subsequent rows: repeat rows 3 and 4 to desired size ending with row 3, then work last row as follows

Last row: 1 ch, turn, dc (US sc) in each st and 5 dc (US sc) in each 5-ch sp across to beginning chain, dc (US sc) in 3rd ch of beginning chain—do not finish off— work 2 rounds of edging in working colour before finishing off.

Double treble/dtr (US treble/tr): YO twice, insert hook in st or sp and pull up a loop, YO and draw through 2 loops on hook 3 times.

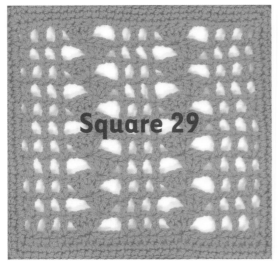

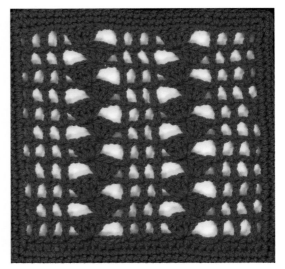

Square 29

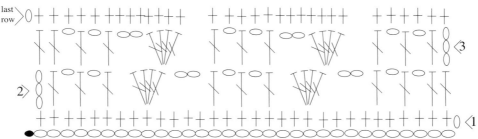

Foundation chain: With Col B make 32 ch.

Row 1: (right side) dc (US sc) in 2nd ch from hook and in each ch across—31 dc (US sc).

Row 2: 3ch [count as tr (US dc) now and throughout, beginning chain], turn, *tr (US dc) in next st, then work [1 ch, skip next st, tr (US dc) in next st] twice, skip next 2 sts, 4 tr (US dc) in next st, 2 ch, skip next 4 sts, repeat from * across ending with tr (US dc) in last st—2 x 4-tr (US dc) shells + 6 x 1-ch sps + 2 x 2-ch sps.

Row 3: 3 ch, turn, *tr (US dc) in next st, work [1 ch, skip next 1-ch sp, tr (US dc) in next st] twice, skip next 2-ch sp, 4 tr (US dc) in next st, 2 ch, skip next 3 sts, repeat from * across ending with tr (US dc) in top of beginning chain—2 x 4-tr (US dc) shells + 6 x 1-ch sps + 2 x 2-ch sps.

Subsequent rows: repeat row 3 to desired size, then work last row as follows.

Last row: 1 ch, turn, dc (US sc) in each st and 1-ch sp and 3 dc (US sc) in each 2-ch sp across to beginning chain, dc (US sc) in top of beginning chain—do not finish off—work 2 rounds of edging in working colour before finishing off.

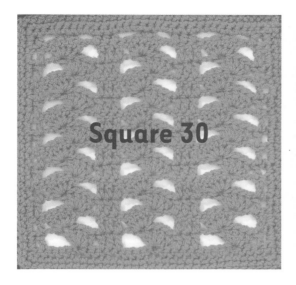

Square 30

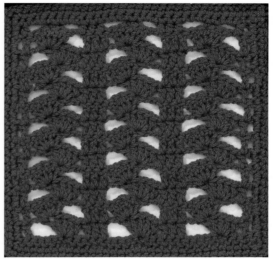

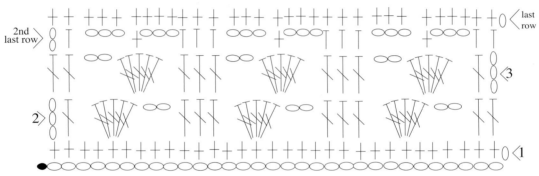

Foundation chain: With Col B make 32 ch.

Row 1: dc (US sc) in 2nd ch from hook and in each ch across—31 dc (US sc).

Row 2: (right side) 3 ch [count as tr (US dc) now and throughout, beginning chain], turn, tr (US dc) in next st, *skip next 2 sts, 5 tr (US dc) in next st (shell made), 2 ch, skip next 4 sts, tr (US dc) in each next 3 sts, repeat from * across to last 2 sts, tr (US dc) in each last 2 sts—3 x shells + 3 x 2-ch sps.

Row 3: 3 ch, turn, tr (US dc) in next st, *5 tr (US dc) in first st of next shell, 2 ch, skip 4 next sts, tr (US dc) in each next 3 sts, repeat from * across ending with tr (US dc) in each last 2 sts—3 x shells + 3 x 2-ch sps.

Subsequent rows: repeat row 3 to desired size, then work 2 last rows as follows

2nd last row: 2 ch [count as htr (US hdc)], turn, htr (US hdc) in next st, *3 ch, dc (US sc) in 3rd st of next shell, 3 ch, skip next 2 sts, htr (US hdc) in each next 3 sts, repeat from * across ending with htr (US hdc) in each last 2 sts—6 x 3-ch sps.

Last row: 1 ch, turn, dc (US sc) in each st and 3 dc (US sc) in each 3-ch sp across to beginning chain, dc (US sc) in 2nd ch of beginning chain—do not finish off— work 2 rounds of edging in working colour before finishing off.

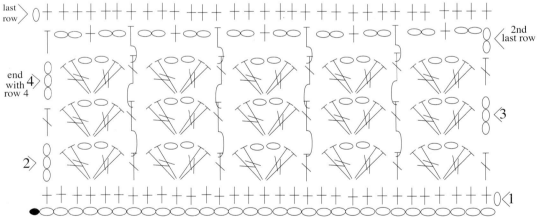

Foundation chain: With Col B make 32 ch.

Row 1: (right side) dc (US sc) in 2nd ch from hook and in each ch across—31 dc (US sc).

Row 2: 3 ch [count as tr (US dc) now and throughout, beginning chain], turn, *skip next 2 sts, in next st work [2 tr (US dc), 2 ch, 2 tr (US dc)], skip next 2 sts, tr (US dc) in next st, repeat from * across—5 x 2-ch sps.

Row 3: 3 ch, turn, *work [2 tr (US dc), 2 ch, 2 tr (US dc)] in next 2-ch sp, skip next 2 sts, work FPtr (US FPdc) around next st, repeat from * across to beginning chain, tr (US dc) in top of beginning chain—5 x 2-ch sps + 4 x FPtr (US FPdc).

Row 4: 3 ch, turn, *work [2 tr (US dc), 2 ch, 2 tr (US dc)] in next 2-ch sp, skip next 2 sts, work BPtr (US BPdc) around next st, repeat from * across to beginning chain, tr (US dc) in top of beginning chain—5 x 2-ch sps + 4 x BPtr (US BPdc).

Subsequent rows: repeat rows 3 and 4 to desired size ending with row 3 or 4, then work 2 last rows as follows.

2nd last row: 4 ch [count as htr (US hdc) + 2-ch sp], turn, *dc (US sc) in next 2-ch sp, 2 ch, skip next 2 sts, (depending on row) work FP or BPhtr (US FPhdc or BPhdc) around next st, 2 ch, repeat from * across to beginning chain, htr (US hdc) in top of beginning chain.

Last row: 1 ch, turn, dc (US sc) in each st and 2 dc (US sc) in each 2-ch sp across to beginning chain, dc (US sc) in 2nd ch of beginning chain—do not finish off—work 2 rounds of edging in working colour before finishing off.

Front post treble/FPtr (US front post double crochet/FPdc): YO, insert hook from front to back around post of stitch indicated, (YO and draw through 2 loops) twice.

Back post treble/BPtr (US back post double crochet/BPdc): YO, insert hook from back to front around post of stitch indicated, (YO and draw through 2 loops) twice.

Front post half treble/FPhtr (US front post half double crochet/FPhdc): YO, insert hook from front to back around post of stitch indicated, YO and draw through 3 loops.

Back post half treble/BPhtr (US bacl post half double crochet/BPhdc): YO, insert hook from back to front around post of stitch indicated, YO and draw through 3 loops.

Square 32

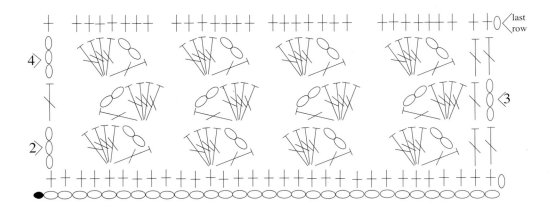

Foundation chain: With Col B make 32 ch.

Row 1: (right side) dc (US sc) in 2nd ch from hook and in each ch across—31 dc (US sc).

Row 2: 3 ch [count as tr (US dc) now and throughout, beginning chain], turn, skip next 3 sts, *in next st work [4 tr (US dc), 2 ch, tr (US dc)], skip next 6 sts, repeat from * across ending with skip next 3 sts and tr (US dc) in each last 2

sts—4 x 2-ch sps.

Row 3: 3 ch, turn, tr (US dc) in next st, *in next 2-ch sp work [4 tr (US dc), 2 ch, tr (US dc)], repeat from * across ending with skip 4 sts and tr (US dc) in top of beginning chain—4 x 2-ch sps.

Row 4: 3 ch, turn, *in next 2-ch sp work [4 tr (US dc), 2 ch, tr (US dc)], repeat from * across ending with skip 4 sts, tr (US dc) in next st and in top of beginning chain—4 x 2-ch sps.

Subsequent rows: repeat rows 3 and 4 to desired size ending with row 4, then work last row as follows.

Last row: 1 ch, turn, dc (US sc) in each st and 2 dc (US sc) in each 2-ch sp across to beginning chain, dc (US sc) in top of of beginning chain—do not finish off—work 2 rounds of edging in working colour before finishing off.

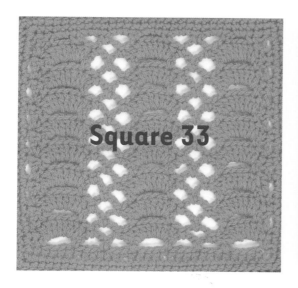

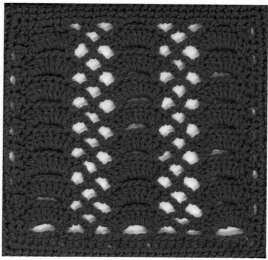

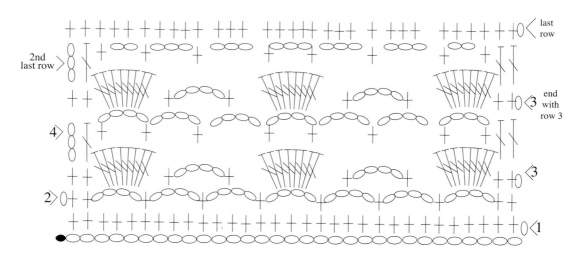

Foundation chain: With Col B make 32 ch.

Row 1: (right side) dc (US sc) in 2nd ch from hook and in each ch across—31 dc (US sc).

Row 2: 1 ch, turn, dc (US sc) in first 2 sts, * 4 ch, skip next 3 sts, dc (US sc) in next st, repeat from * across ending with dc (US sc) in last st—7 x 4-ch sps.

Row 3: 1 ch, turn, dc (US sc) in first 2 sts, *8 tr (US dc) in next 4-ch sp (fan made), dc (US sc) in next 4-ch sp, 4 ch, dc (US sc) in next 4-ch sp, repeat from * across ending with dc (US sc) in each last 2 sts—3 x fans + 2 x 4-ch sps.

Row 4: 3 ch [count as tr (US dc), now and throughout, beginning chain], tr (US dc) in next st, *skip next tr (US dc), dc (US sc) in next st, 4 ch, skip next 4 sts, dc (US sc) in next st, 4 ch, dc (US sc) in next 4-ch sp, 4 ch, repeat from * across ending with tr (US dc) in each last 2 sts—7 x 4-ch sps.

Subsequent rows: repeat rows 3 and 4 to desired size ending with row 3, then work 2 last rows as follows.

2nd last row: 3 ch, turn, tr (US dc) in next st, skip next tr (US dc), dc (US sc) in next st, 2 ch, *skip 4 sts, dc (US sc) in next st, 3 ch, dc (US sc) in next 4-ch sp, 3 ch, skip next tr (US dc), dc (US sc) in next st, 3 ch, repeat from * across ending with 2 ch, skip next 4 sts, dc (US sc) in next st and tr (US dc) in each last 2 sts—10 x 2-ch sps.

Last row: 1 ch, turn, dc (US sc) in each st, 2 dc (US sc) in each 2-ch sp and 3 dc (US sc) in each 3-ch sp across—do not finish off—work 2 rounds of edging in working colour before finishing off.

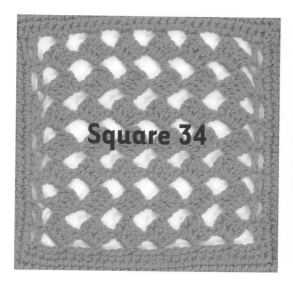

Square 34

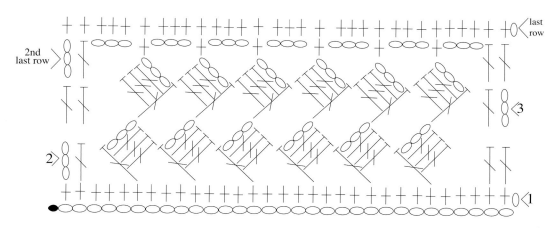

Foundation chain: With Col B make 32 ch.

Row 1: (right side) dc (US sc) in 2nd ch from hook and in each ch across—31 dc (US sc).

Row 2: 3 ch [count as tr (US dc) now and throughout, beginning chain], turn, tr (US dc) in next st, *skip next 3 sts, tr (US dc) in next st, working over tr (US dc) just made work [3 ch, 3 tr (US dc)] (shell made), repeat from * across ending with tr (US dc) in each last 2 sts—6 x shells.

Row 3: 3 ch, turn, tr (US dc) in next st, *tr (US dc) in next shell (in top of 3 ch), work shell over tr (US dc) just made, repeat from * across ending with tr (US dc) in last 2 sts—6 x shells.

Subsequent rows: repeat row 3 to desired size, then work 2 last rows as follows.

2nd last row: 3 ch, turn, tr (US dc) in next st, *3 ch, dc (US sc) in next shell, repeat from * ending with tr (US dc) in each last 2 sts.

Last row: 1 ch, turn, dc (US sc) in each st and 3 dc (US sc) in each 3-ch sp—do not finish off—work 2 rounds of edging in working colour before finishing off.

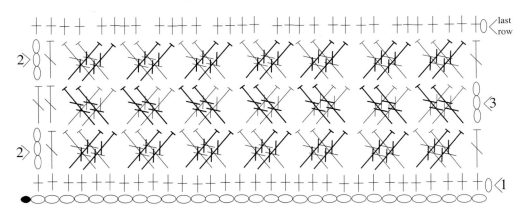

Foundation chain: With Col B make 32 ch.

Row 1: (right side) dc (US sc) in 2nd ch from hook and in each ch across—31 dc (US sc).

Row 2: 3 ch [count as tr (US dc), now and throughout, beginning chain], turn, tr (US dc) in next st, *skip next 2 sts, dtr (US tr) in each next 2 sts, work [whff] dtr (US tr) in each skipped st, repeat from * across ending with tr (US dc) in last st—11 x tr (US dc) + 5 x crossed dtr (US tr) groups.

Row 3: 3 ch, turn, *skip next 2 sts, dtr (US tr) in each next 2 sts, work [whff] dtr (US tr) in each skipped st, repeat from * across ending with tr (US dc) in each last 2 sts—11 x tr (US dc) + 5 x crossed dtr (US tr) groups.

Subsequent rows: repeat rows 2 and 3 to desired size, then work last row as follows.

Last row: 1 ch, turn, dc (US sc) in each st across—do not finish off—work 2 rounds of edging in working colour before finishing off.

Note: [whff] = work hook from front.

Double treble/dtr (US treble/tr): YO twice, insert hook in st or sp and draw up a loop, YO and draw through 2 loops on hook 3 times.

Square 36

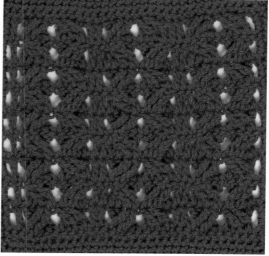

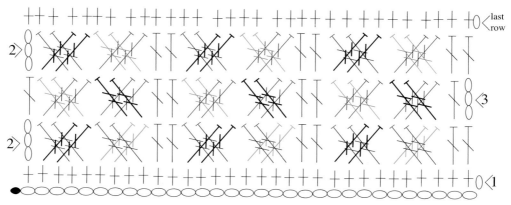

Foundation chain: With Col B make 32 ch.

Row 1: dc (US sc) in 2nd ch from hook and in each ch across—31 dc (US sc).

Row 2: (right side) 3 ch [count as tr (US dc) now and throughout, beginning chain], turn, *skip next 2 sts, dtr (US tr) in each next 2 sts, work [whff] dtr (US tr) in each skipped st, skip next 2 sts, dtr (US tr) in next 2 sts, work [whfb] dtr (US tr) in each skipped st, tr (US dc) in each next 2 sts, repeat from * across—3 x [whff] crossed dtr (US tr) groups + 3 x [whfb] crossed dtr (US tr) groups + 7 x tr (US dc).

Row 3: 3 ch, turn, tr (US dc) in next st, *skip next 2 sts, dtr (US tr) in each next 2 sts, work [whff] dtr (US tr) in each skipped st, skip 2 sts, dtr (US tr) in next 2 sts, work [whfb] dtr (US tr) in each skipped st, tr (US dc) in each next 2 sts, repeat from * across ending with tr (US dc) in last st—3 x [whff] crossed dtr (US tr) groups + 3 x [whfb] crossed dtr (US tr) groups + 7 x tr (US dc).

Subsequent rows: repeat rows 2 and 3 to desired size, then work last row as follows.

Last row: 1 ch, turn, dc (US sc) in each st across—do not finish off—work 2 rounds of edging in working colour before finishing off.

Note: [whff] = work hook from front (indicated by darker symbols in diagram)

Note: [whfb] = work hook from back (indicated by red symbols in diagram)

Double treble/dtr (US treble/tr): YO twice, insert hook in st or sp and draw up a loop, YO and draw through 2 loops on hook 3 times.

Square 37

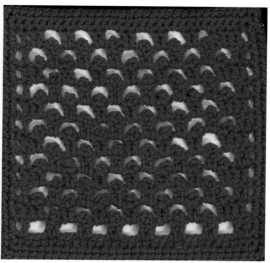

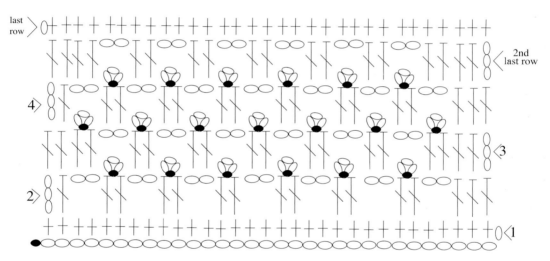

Foundation chain: With Col B make 32 ch.

Row 1: (right side) dc (US sc) in 2nd ch from hook and in each ch across—31 dc (US sc).

Row 2: 3 ch [count as tr (US dc) now and throughout, beginning chain], turn, tr (US dc) in next st, *2 ch, skip next 2 sts, in next st work [tr (US dc), picot], tr (US dc) in next st, repeat from * across ending with tr (US dc) in each last 3 sts—6 x picots.

Row 3: 3 ch, turn, tr (US dc) in each next 2 sts, *in next 2-ch sp work [tr (US dc), picot, tr (US dc)], 2 ch, repeat from * across ending with tr (US dc) in each last 2 sts—7 x picots.

Row 4: 3 ch, turn, tr (US dc) in next st, 2 ch, *in next 2-ch sp work [tr (US dc), picot, tr (US dc)], 2 ch, repeat from * across ending with tr (US dc) in each last 3 sts—6 x picots.

Subsequent rows: repeat rows 3 and 4 to desired size ending with row 4, then work 2 last rows as follows.

2nd last row: 3 ch, turn, tr (US dc) in each next 2 sts, *2 tr (US dc) in next 2-ch sp, 2 ch, 2 tr (US dc) in next 2-ch sp, 2 ch, repeat from * across ending with tr (US dc) in each last 3 sts—19 x tr (US dc).

Last row: 1 ch, turn, dc (US sc) in each st and 2 dc (US sc) in each 2-ch sp across—do not finish off—work 2 rounds of edging in working colour before finishing off.

Picot: 3 ch, ss in tr (US dc) just made (for best results work picot tightly).

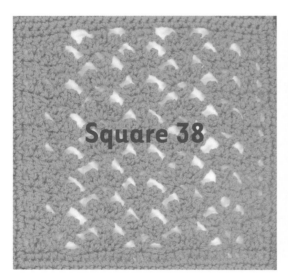

Square 38

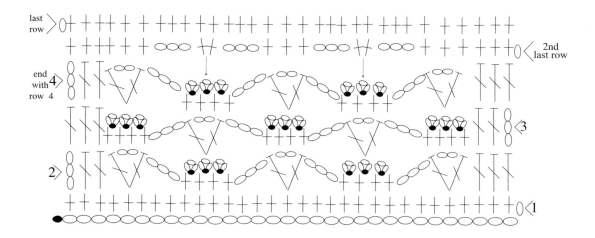

Foundation chain: With Col B make 32 ch.

Row 1: (right side) dc (US sc) in 2nd ch from hook and in each ch across—31 dc (US sc).

Row 2: 3 ch [count as tr (US dc) now and throughout, beginning chain], turn, tr (US dc) in next 2 sts, skip next st, *in next st work [tr (US dc), 2 ch, tr (US dc)] (V-st made), 2 ch, skip next 3 sts, [dc (US sc) in next st, picot] 3 times, in next st work [dc (US sc), 2 ch], skip next 3 sts**, repeat from * to ** across to last 4 sts, skip next st and tr (US dc) in each last 3 sts—3 x V-st + 6 x picots.

Row 3: 3 ch, turn tr (US dc) in next 2 sts, *in next st work [dc (US sc), picot], in next 2-ch sp work [dc (US sc), picot] twice, in next st work [dc (US sc), 2 ch], skip next 2-ch sp and next picot, in next picot work (V-st, 2 ch), skip next picot

and 2-ch sp, repeat from * across ending with tr (US dc) in each last 3 sts—2 x V-st + 9 x picots.

Row 4: 3 ch, turn, tr (US dc) in next 2 sts, skip next picot, *in next picot work (V-st, 2 ch), skip next picot and 2-ch sp, in next st work [dc (US sc), picot], in next 2-ch sp work [dc (US sc), picot] twice, in next st work [dc (US sc), 2 ch], skip next 2-ch sp and next picot, in next picot work (V-st, 2 ch), repeat from * across ending with tr (US dc) in each last 3 sts—3 x V-st + 6 x picots.

Subsequent rows: repeat rows 3 and 4 to desired size ending with row 4, then work 2 last rows as follows.

2nd last row: 1 ch, turn, dc (US sc) in first 4 sts, dc (US sc) in next 2-ch sp, dc (US sc) in next st, *3 ch, skip next 2-ch sp and next picot, 2 dc (US sc) in next picot, 3 ch, skip next picot and 2-ch sp, dc (US sc) in each next st, 2-ch sp and st, repeat from * ending with dc (US sc) in last 3 sts—4 x 3-ch sps + 19 x dc (US sc).

Last row: 1 ch, turn, dc (US sc) in each st and 3 dc (US sc) in each 3-ch

sp across—do not finish off—work 2 rounds of edging in working colour before finishing off.

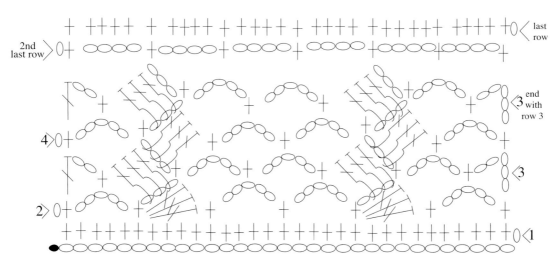 **Picot:** 3 ch, ss in 3rd ch from hook (for best results work picot tightly).

Square 39

Foundation chain: With Col B make 32 ch.

Row 1: (right side) dc (US sc) in 2nd ch from hook and in each ch across—31 dc (US sc).

Row 2: 1 ch, turn, dc (US sc) in first st, 5 ch, *skip 4 sts, in next st work [dc (US sc), 3 ch, 3 tr (US dc)]**, [skip 4 sts, dc (US sc) in next st, 5 ch] twice, repeat from * to ** once, ending with skip 4 sts, dc (US sc) in next st, 5 ch, skip 4 sts, dc (US sc) in last st—2 x shells + 4 x 5-ch sps.

Row 3: 5 ch [count as tr (US dc) + 2-ch sp, now and throughout, beginning chain], turn, dc (US sc) in next 5-ch sp, 5 ch, *dc (US sc) in top of 3 ch of previous row, 3 ch, work 3 tr (US dc) around 3-ch of previous row**, [dc (US sc) in next 5-ch sp, 5 ch] twice, repeat from * to ** once, ending with dc (US sc) in next 5-ch sp, 2 ch, tr (US dc) in last st—2 x 4-tr (US dc) shells + 2 x shells + 2 x 2-ch sps + 3 x 3-ch sps.

Row 4: 1 ch, turn, dc (US sc) in first st, 5 ch, *dc (US sc) in top of 3 ch of previous row, 3 ch, work 3 tr (US dc) around 3 ch of previous row**, [dc (US sc) in next st, 5 ch] twice, repeat from * to ** once, ending with dc (US sc) in next 5-ch sp, 5 ch, dc (US sc) in 3rd ch of beginning chain—2 x shells + 4 x 5-ch sps.

Subsequent rows: repeat rows 3 and 4 to desired size ending with row 3, then work 2 rows as follows.

2nd last row: 1 ch, turn, dc (US sc) in first st, *4 ch, dc (US sc) in top of 3-ch of previous row**, [4 ch, dc (US sc) in next 5-ch sp] twice, repeat from * to ** ending with 4 ch, dc (US sc) in next 5-ch sp, 4 ch and dc (US sc) in 3rd ch of beginning chain—6 x 4-ch sps.

Last row: 1 ch, turn, dc (US sc) in each st and 4 dc (US sc) in each 4-ch sp across—do not finish off—work 2 rounds of edging in working colour before finishing off.

Square 40

Foundation chain: With Col B make 32 ch.

Row 1: (right side) dc (US sc) in 2nd ch from hook and in each ch across—31 dc (US sc).

Row 2: 3 ch [count as tr (US dc) now and throughout, beginning chain], turn, *tr (US dc) in next st, work FPtr (US FPdc) around last st just made, skip next st, repeat from * across ending with, tr (US dc) in each last 2 sts—14 x FPtr (US FPdc) + 3 x tr (US dc).

Subsequent rows: repeat row 2 to desired size, then work last row as follows.

Last row: 1 ch, turn, dc (US sc) in each st across—do not finish off—work 2 rounds of edging in working colour before finishing off.

Front post treble/FPtr (US front post double crochet/FPdc):
    YO, insert hook from front to back around post of stitch indicated, (YO and draw through 2 loops) twice.

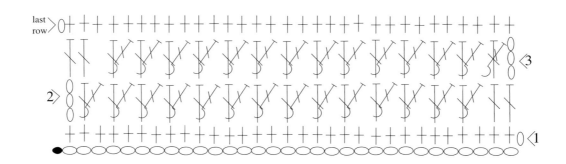

Square 41

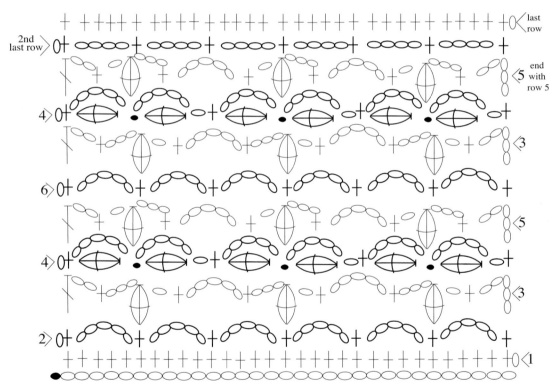

Foundation chain: With Col B make 32 ch.

Row 1: (right side) dc (US sc) in 2nd ch from hook and in each ch across—31 dc (US sc).

Row 2: 1 ch, turn, dc (US sc) in first st, *5 ch, skip next 4 sts, dc (US sc) in next st, repeat from * across—6 x 5-ch sps.

Row 3: 5 ch [count as tr (US dc) + 2 ch, now and throughout, beginning chain], turn, *in next 5-ch sp work [dc (US sc), 1 ch], in next dc (US sc) work (CL, 3 ch), in next 5-ch sp work [dc (US sc), 5 ch], repeat from * across ending with dc (US sc) in last 5-ch sp, 2 ch and tr (US dc) in last st—3 x cluster + 2 x 3-ch sps + 2 x 5-ch sps.

Row 4: 1 ch, turn, dc (US sc) in first st, *from same st work [5 ch, CL, ss into top of next CL of previous row, then from same ss work (5 ch, CL, 1 ch)], dc (US sc) in next 5-ch sp, repeat from * across ending with dc (US sc) in 3rd ch of beginning chain—6 x cluster + 6 x 5-ch sps.

Row 5: 5 ch, turn, *in next 5-ch sp work [dc (US sc), 3 ch] in next 5-ch sp, in ss of previous row work (CL, 1 ch), in next 5-ch sp work [dc (US sc), 5 ch], repeat from * across ending with dc (US sc) in last 5-ch sp, 2 ch and tr (US dc) in last st—3 x cluster + 2 x 3-ch sps + 2 x 5-ch sps.

Row 6: 1 ch, turn, dc (US sc) in first st, *5 ch, dc (US sc) in next 3-ch sp, 5 ch,

dc (US sc) in next 5-ch sp, repeat from * across ending with working last dc (US sc) in 3rd ch of beginning chain—6 x 5-ch sps.

Subsequent rows: repeat row 3 to 6 to desired size ending with row 5, then work 2 last rows as follows.

2nd last row: 1 ch, turn, dc (US sc) in first st, *4 ch, dc (US sc) in next 3-ch sp, 4 ch, dc (US sc) in next 5-ch sp, repeat from * across ending with dc (US sc) in 3rd ch of beginning chain—6 x 5-ch sps.

Last row: 1 ch, turn, dc (US sc) in each st and 4 dc (US sc) in each 4-ch sp across—do not finish off—work 2 rounds of edging in working colour before finishing off.

Cluster: (YO, insert hook in stitch or space indicated and pull up a loop, YO and draw through 2 loops on hook) 3 times, YO and draw through all 4 loops on hook.

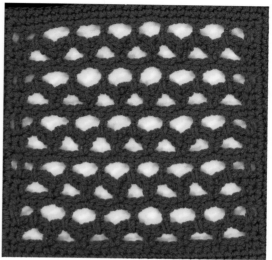

Square 42

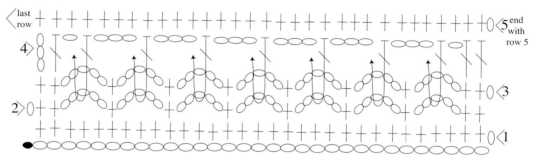

Foundation chain: With Col B make 32 ch.

Row 1: (right side) dc (US sc) in 2nd ch from hook and in each ch across—31 dc (US sc).

Row 2: 1 ch, turn, dc (US sc) in first 2 sts, *5 ch, skip 3 sts, dc (US sc) in next st, repeat from * across ending with dc (US sc) in last st—7 x 5-ch sps.

Row 3: 1 ch, turn, dc (US sc) in first 2 sts, *5 ch, dc (US sc) in next dc (US sc), repeat from * across ending with dc (US sc) in last st—7 x 5-ch sps.

Row 4: 3 ch [count as tr (US dc) now and throughout, beginning chain], turn, tr (US dc) in next st, 1 ch, *work tr (US dc) over both 5-ch loops of previous 2 rows, 3 ch, repeat from * across ending with 1 ch and tr (US dc) in each last 2 sts—6 x 3-ch sps + 1 x 1-ch sps.

Row 5: 1 ch, turn dc (US sc) in each st and 1-ch sp and 3 dc (US sc) in each 3-ch sp across—31 dc (US sc).

Subsequent rows: repeat rows 2 to 5 to desired size ending with row 5—do not finish off—work 2 rounds of edging in working colour before finishing off.

Square 43

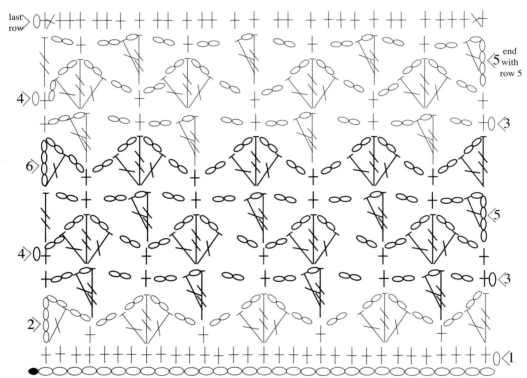

Foundation chain: With Col B make 32 ch.

Row 1: (right side) dc (US sc) in 2nd ch from hook and in each ch across—31 dc (US sc).

Row 2: 6 ch [count as dtr (US tr) + 2 ch, now and throughout, beginning chain], turn, tr (US dc) in same st, 2 ch, skip next 2 sts, dc (US sc) in next st, *2 ch, skip next 3 sts, in next st work [tr (US dc), 2 ch, dtr (US tr), 2 ch, tr (US dc)], 2 ch, skip next 3 sts, dc (US sc) in next st, repeat from * across ending with 2 ch, skip 2 sts and [tr (US dc), 2 ch, dtr (US tr)] in last st—16 x 2-ch sps.

Row 3: 1 ch, turn, dc (US sc) in first st, *2 ch, in next dc (US sc) work [dtr (US tr), 1 ch], work tr (US dc) in side of st just made, 2 ch, dc (US sc) in next dtr (US tr), repeat from * across ending with 2 ch and dc (US sc) in 4th ch of beginning chain—8 x 2-ch sps + 4 x 1-ch sps.

Row 4: 1 ch, turn, dc (US sc) in first st, *2 ch, in next 1-ch sp work [tr (US dc), 2 ch, dtr (US tr), 2 ch, tr (US dc)], 2 ch, dc (US sc) in next dc (US sc), repeat from * across—16 x 2-ch sps.

Row 5: 5 ch [count as dtr (US tr) + 1 ch, now and throughout, beginning chain], work tr (US dc) in 2nd ch of 5-ch beginning ch just made, *2 ch, dc (US sc) in next dtr (US tr), 2 ch, [dtr (US tr), 1 ch] in next dc (US sc), work tr (US dc) in side of st just made, repeat from * across

ending with 2 ch, dtr (US tr) in last st—8 x 2-ch sps + 4 x 1-ch sps.

Row 6: 6 ch, turn, tr (US dc) in same st, *2 ch, dc (US sc) in next dc (US sc), 2 ch, in next 1-ch sp work [tr (US dc), 2 ch, dtr (US tr), 2 ch, tr (US dc)], repeat from * across ending with 2 ch and [tr (US dc), 2 ch, dtr (US tr)] in 4th ch of beginning chain—5 x 5-ch sps + 16 x 2-ch sps.

Subsequent rows: repeat rows 3 to 6 to desired size ending with row 5, then work last row as follows.

Last row: 1 ch, turn, 2 dc (US sc) in first st, dc (US sc) in each st and 2 dc (US sc) in each 2-ch sp across ending with 2 dc (US sc) in 4th ch of beginning chain (leaving 1-ch sps unused)—do not finish off—work 2 rounds of edging in working colour before finishing off.

Double treble/dtr (US treble/tr): YO twice, insert hook in st or sp and pull up a loop, YO and draw through 2 loops on hook 3 times.

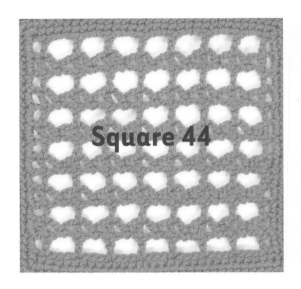

Square 44

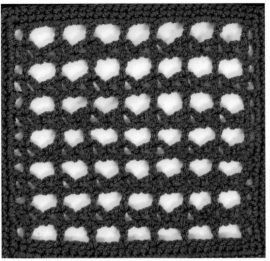

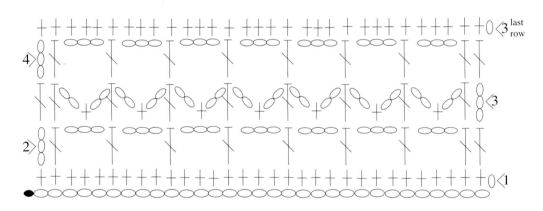

Foundation chain: With Col C make 32 ch.

Row 1: (right side) dc (US sc) in 2nd ch from hook and in each ch across—31 dc (US sc).

Row 2: 3 ch [count as tr (US dc) now and throughout, beginning chain], turn, tr (US dc) in next st, *3 ch, skip next 3 sts, tr (US dc) in next st, repeat from * across ending with tr (US dc) in each last 2 sts—10 x tr (US dc) + 7 x 3-ch sps.

Row 3: 3 ch, turn, tr (US dc) in next st, *2 ch, dc (US sc) in next 3-ch sp, 2 ch, tr (US dc) in next st, repeat from * across ending with tr (US dc) in last st—10 x tr (US dc) + 14 x 2-ch sps.

Row 4: 3 ch, turn, tr (US dc) in next st, *3 ch, tr (US dc) in next tr (US dc), repeat from * across ending with tr (US dc) in each last 2 sts—10 x tr (US dc) + 7 x 3-ch sps.

Subsequent rows: repeat rows 3 and 4 to desired size ending with row 4, then work last row as follows.

Last row: 1 ch, turn, dc (US sc) in each st and 3 dc (US sc) in each 3-ch sp across—do not finish off—work 2 rounds of edging in working colour before finishing off.

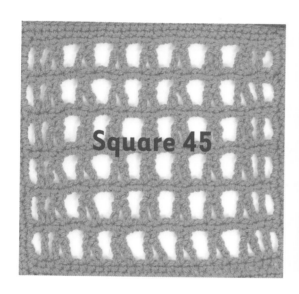

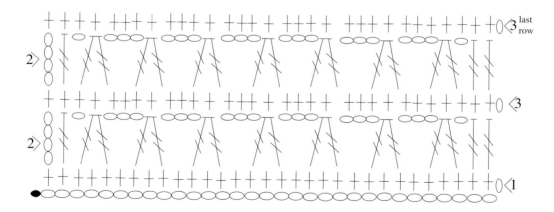

Foundation chain: With Col C make 32 ch.

Row 1: dc (US sc) in 2nd ch from hook and in each ch across—31 dc (US sc).

Row 2: (right side) 4 ch [count as dtr (US tr), now and throughout, beginning chain], turn, dtr (US tr) in next st, 1 ch, *work CL over next 3 sts, 3 ch, skip next st, repeat from * across ending with 1 ch and dtr (US tr) in each last 2 sts—7 x CL+ 6 x 3-ch sps + 2 x 1-ch sps.

Row 3: 1 ch, turn, dc (US sc) in each st and 1-ch sp and 3 dc (US sc) in each 3-ch sp across—31 dc (US sc).

Subsequent rows: repeat rows 2 and 3 to desired size ending with row 3—do not finish off—work 2 rounds of edging in working colour before finishing off.

Double treble/dtr (US treble/tr): YO twice, insert hook in st or sp and pull up a loop, YO and draw through 2 loops on hook 3 times.

Cluster (CL): [(*YO twice, insert hook in first st indicated and draw up a loop, YO and draw through 2 loops twice **), skip next st, then repeat from * to **], YO and draw through 3 loops on hook.

Square 46

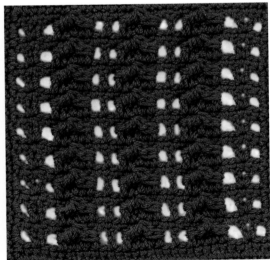

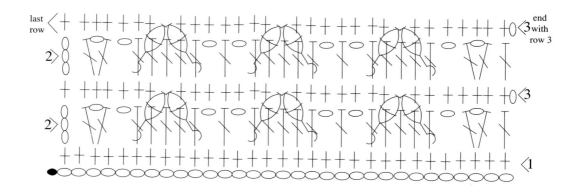

Foundation chain: With Col C make 32 ch.

Row 1: (right side) dc (US sc) in 2nd ch from hook and in each ch across—31 dc (US sc).

Row 2: 3 ch [count as tr (US dc), now and throughout, beginning chain], turn, skip next st, in next st work [tr (US dc), 1 ch, tr (US dc)] (V-st made), 1 ch, skip 2 sts, *tr (US dc) in each next 5 sts, 1 ch, skip next st, tr (US dc) in next st, 1 ch, skip next st, repeat from * across to last 5 sts and ending with 1 ch, skip 2 sts, V-st in next st, skip next st, tr (US dc) in last st—2 x V-st + 3 x 5-tr (US dc) group.

Row 3: 1 ch, turn, dc (US sc) in first st, [dc (US sc) in next st and 1-ch sp] twice, *dc (US sc) in next 2 sts, work FPDCL over first and 5th st of same 5-st group

(leaving st behind FPDCL just made unused), dc (US sc) in next 2 sts of same 5-st group, dc (US sc) in next 1-ch sp, dc (US sc) in next st, dc (US sc) in next 1-ch sp, repeat from * across to last 5 sts, [dc (US sc) in next 1-ch sp and next st] twice, dc (US sc) on top of beginning chain.

Subsequent rows: repeat rows 2 and 3 to desired size ending with row 3—do not finish off—work 2 rounds of edging in working colour before finishing off.

Front post double cluster/ FPDCL: (*YO, insert hook from front to back around post of first st indicated and draw up a loop, YO and draw through 2 loops) twice** (3 loops on hook), repeat from * to ** around 5th st of same st group (5 loops on hook), YO and draw through all 5 loops.

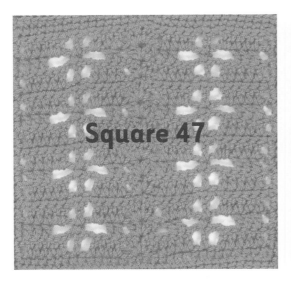

Square 47

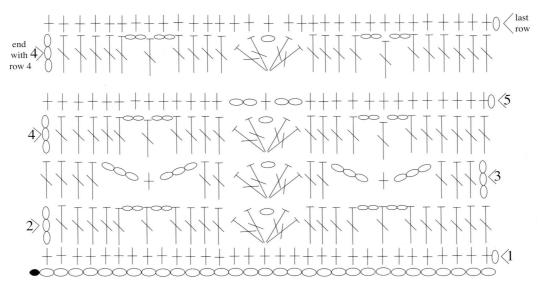

Foundation chain: With Col C make 32 ch.

Row 1: (right side) dc (US sc) in 2nd ch from hook and in each ch across—31 dc (US sc).

Row 2: 3 ch [count as tr (US dc), now and throughout, beginning chain],

turn, tr (US dc) in next 5 sts, 2 ch, skip next st, tr (US dc) in next st, 2 ch, skip next st, tr (US dc) in next 4 sts, skip next 2 sts, in next st work [2 tr (US dc), 1 ch, 2 tr (US dc)] (shell made), skip next 2 sts, tr (US dc) in next 4 sts, 2 ch, skip next st, tr (US dc) in next st, 2 ch, skip next st, tr (US dc) in last 6 sts—4 x 2-ch sps + 1 x shell + 22 x tr (US dc).

Row 3: 3 ch, turn, tr (US dc) in next 3 sts, *3 ch, skip 2 sts and 2-ch sp, dc (US sc) in next st, 3 ch, skip next 2-ch sp and next 2 sts**, tr (US dc) in next 2 sts, work shell in 1-ch sp of next shell, skip 2nd half of shell, tr (US dc) in next 2 sts, repeat from * to ** once more, ending with tr (US dc) in last 4 sts—4 x 3-ch sps + 1 x shell + 12 x tr (US dc) + 2 x dc (US sc).

Row 4: 3 ch, turn, tr (US dc) in next 3 sts and 2 tr (US dc) in next 3-ch sp, 2 ch, tr (US dc) in next st, 2 ch, 2 tr (US dc) in next 3-ch sp and in each next 2 sts, work shell in 1-ch sp of next shell, skip 2nd half of shell, tr (US dc) in each next 2 sts and 2 tr (US dc) in next 3-ch sp, 2 ch, tr (US dc) in next st, 2 ch, 2 tr (US dc) in next 3-ch sp and in each last 4 sts—4 x 2-ch sps + 1 x shell + 22 x tr (US dc).

Row 5: 1 ch, turn, dc (US sc) in each [first 6 sts, 2-ch sp, tr (US dc), 2-ch sp and next 4 sts], 2 ch (count as 2 sts), dc (US sc) in 1-ch sp of next shell, skip 2nd half of shell, 2 ch, dc (US sc) in each st and 2-ch sp across to end—27 x dc (US sc) + 2 x 2-ch sps.

Subsequent rows: repeat rows 2 to 5 to desired size ending with row 4, then work last row as follows.

Last row: 1 ch, turn, dc (US sc) in each st, 1-ch sp and 2-ch sp across—do not finish off—work 2 rounds of edging in working colour before finishing off.

Square 48

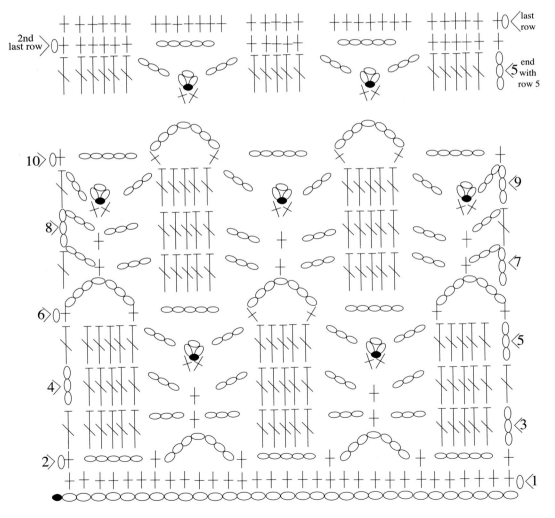

Foundation chain: With Col C make 32 ch.

Row 1: (right side) dc (US sc) in 2nd ch from hook and in each ch across—31 dc (US sc).

Row 2: 1 ch, turn, dc (US sc) in first st, *5 ch, skip next 5 sts, dc (US sc) in next st, 7 ch, skip next 5 sts, dc (US sc) in next st, repeat from * across—3 x 5-ch sps + 2 x 7-ch sps.

Row 3: 3 ch [count as tr (US dc) now and throughout, beginning chain], *work 5 tr (US dc) in next 5-ch sp, in next 7-ch sp work [3 ch, dc (US sc), 3 ch], repeat from * across ending with tr (US dc) in last st—4 x 3-ch sps + 3 x 5-tr (US dc) groups.

Row 4: 3 ch, *tr (US dc) in each next 5 sts, 3 ch, dc (US sc) in next st, 3 ch, repeat from * across ending with tr (US dc) in top of beginning chain—4 x 3-ch sps.

Row 5: 3 ch, *tr (US dc) in next 5 sts, 3 ch, [dc (US sc), picot, dc (US sc)] in next st, 3 ch, repeat from * across ending with tr (US dc) in top of beginning chain—4 x 3-ch sps + 2 x picots.

Row 6: 1 ch, turn, dc (US sc) in first st, *7 ch, skip next 4 sts, dc (US sc) in next st, 5 ch, dc (US sc) in next tr (US dc), 7 ch, skip 3 sts, dc (US sc) in next st, 5 ch, dc (US sc) in next tr (US dc), 7 ch, dc (US sc) in top of beginning chain—3 x 7-ch sps + 2 x 5-ch sps.

Row 7: 6 ch [count as tr (US dc) + 3 ch, now and throughout, beginning chain], in next 7-ch sp work [dc (US sc), 3 ch], *work 5 tr (US dc) in next 5-ch sp, in next 7-ch sp work [3ch, dc (US sc), 3 ch]**, repeat from * to ** once more, ending with tr (US dc) in last st—6 x 3-ch sps.

Row 8: 6 ch, *in next dc (US sc) work [dc (US sc), 3 ch], tr (US dc) in next 5 sts, 3 ch, repeat from * across ending with tr (US dc) in 3rd ch of beginning chain—6 x 3-ch sps.

Row 9: 6 ch, in next dc (US sc) work [dc (US sc), picot, dc (US sc), 3 ch], *tr (US dc) in next 5 sts, in next 7-ch sp work [3 ch, dc (US sc), picot, 3 ch], repeat from * across ending with tr (US dc) in 3rd ch of beginning chain—6 x 3-ch sps + 3 x picots.

Row 10: 1 ch, turn, dc (US sc) in first st, *5 ch, dc (US sc) in next tr (US dc), 7 ch, skip 3 sts, dc (US sc) in next st, repeat from * across ending with dc (US sc) in 3rd ch of beginning chain—3 x 5-ch sps + 2 x 7-ch sps.

Subsequent rows: repeat rows 3 to 5 once more, then work 2 last rows as follows.

2nd last row: 1 ch, turn, dc (US sc) in first 6 sts, 5 ch, *dc (US sc) in next 5 sts, 5 ch, dc (US sc) in next 5 sts, repeat from * across ending with dc (US sc) in top of beginning chain—17 x dc (US sc) + 2 x 5-ch sps.

Last row: 1 ch, turn, dc (US sc) in each st and 7 dc (US sc) in each 5-ch sp across—do not finish off—work 2 rounds of edging in working colour before finishing off.

 Picot: 3 ch, ss in 3rd ch from hook (for best results work picot tightly).

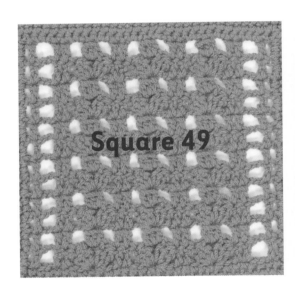

Square 49

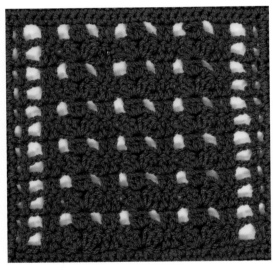

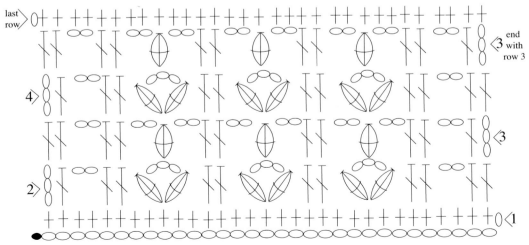

Foundation chain: With Col C make 32 ch.

Row 1: (right side) dc (US sc) in 2nd ch from hook and in each ch across—31 dc (US sc).

Row 2: 3 ch [count as tr (US dc) now and throughout, beginning chain], turn, tr (US dc) in next st, 2 ch, *skip next 2 sts, tr (US dc) in each next 2 sts, skip next 2 sts, in next st work (CL, 3 ch, CL), repeat from * across ending with 2 ch, skip 2 sts, tr (US dc) in each last 2 sts—3 x cluster group + 12 x tr (US dc) + 2 x 2-ch sps.

Row 3: 3 ch, tr (US dc) in next st, 2 ch, *tr (US dc) in each next 2 sts, 2 ch, work CL in next 3-ch sp, 2 ch, repeat from * across ending with 2 ch, tr (US dc) in last 2 sts—3 x clusters + 12 x tr (US dc) + 8 x 2-ch sps.

Row 4: 3 ch, turn, tr (US dc) in next st, 2 ch, *tr (US dc) in each next 2 sts, in top of next CL work (CL, 3 ch, CL), repeat from * across ending with 2 ch, tr (US dc) in each last 2 sts—3 x clusters + 12 x tr (US dc) + 2 x 2-ch sps.

Subsequent rows: repeat rows 3 and 4 to desired size ending with row 3, then work last row as follows.

Last row: 1 ch, turn, dc (US sc) in each st and 2 dc (US sc) in each 2-ch sp across—do not finish off—work 2 rounds of edging in working colour before finishing off.

Cluster (CL): (YO, insert hook in stitch or space indicated and pull up a loop, YO and draw through 2 loops on hook) 3 times, YO and draw through all 4 loops on hook.

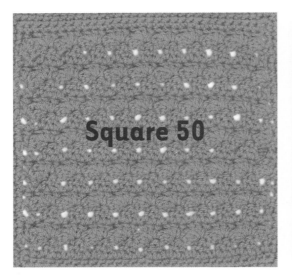

Square 50

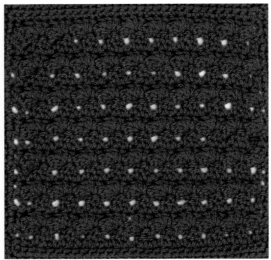

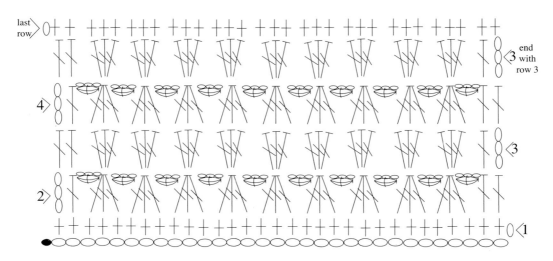

This is a wide pattern; work more tightly than usual or go down a hook size.

Foundation chain: With Col C make 32 ch.

Row 1: (right side) dc (US sc) in 2nd ch from hook and in each ch across—31 dc (US sc).

Row 2: 3 ch [count as tr (US dc) now and throughout, beginning chain], turn, tr (US dc) in next st, *3 ch, work CL(1) in top of st just made, work CL(2) over next 3 sts, repeat from * across to last 2 sts, tr (US dc) in last 2 sts—10 x CL(1) + 9 x CL(2).

Row 3: 3 ch, turn, tr (US dc) in next st, *3 tr (US dc) in top of next CL(2), repeat from * across to last 2 sts, tr (US dc) in each last 2 sts—9 x 3 tr (US dc) groups.

Row 4: 3 ch, turn, tr (US dc) in next st, *3 ch, work CL(1) in top of st just made, work CL(2) over next 3 sts, repeat from * across to last 2 sts, tr (US dc) in last 2 sts—10 x CL(1) + 9 x CL(2).

Subsequent rows: repeat rows 3 and 4 to desired size ending with row 3, then work last row as follows

Last row: 1 ch, turn, dc (US sc) in each st across to beginning chain, dc (US sc) in top of beginning chain—do not finish off—work 2 rounds of edging in working colour before finishing off.

Cluster 1/CL(1): (YO, insert hook in stitch or space indicated and pull up a loop, YO and draw through 2 loops on hook) twice, YO and draw through all 3 loops on hook.

Cluster 2/CL(2): (YO, insert hook in st indicated and draw up a loop, YO and draw through 2 loops) repeat over number of sts indicated, YO and draw through all 4 loops on hook.

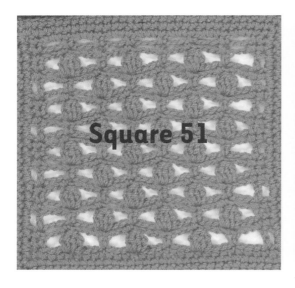

Square 51

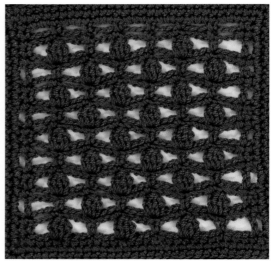

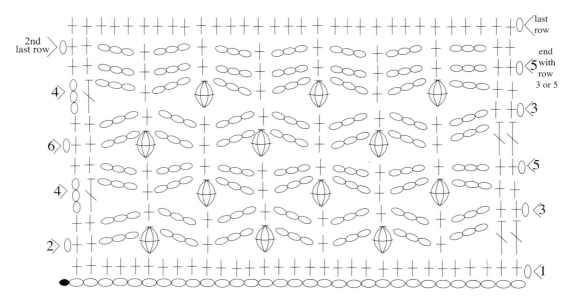

Foundation chain: With Col C make 32 ch.

Row 1: (right side) dc (US sc) in 2nd ch from hook and in each ch across—31 dc (US sc).

Row 2: 1 ch, turn dc (US sc) in first 2 sts, *3 ch, skip next 3 sts, work CL in next st, 3 ch, skip next 3 sts, dc (US sc) in next st, repeat from * across ending with tr (US dc) in each last 2 sts—3 x clusters + 5 x 3-ch sps + 2 x tr (US dc).

Row 3: 1 ch, turn dc (US sc) in first 2 sts, *3 ch, dc (US sc) in next dc (US sc), 3 ch, dc (US sc) in next CL, repeat from * across ending with dc (US sc) in last st—10 x dc (US sc) + 7 x 3-ch sps.

Row 4: 3 ch [count as tr (US dc) now and throughout, beginning chain], tr (US dc) in next st, *3 ch, dc (US sc) in next dc (US sc), 3 ch, work CL in next dc (US sc), repeat from * across ending with dc (US sc) in last st—2 x tr (US dc) + 3 x clusters + 7 x 3-ch sps.

Row 5: 1 ch, turn, dc (US sc) in first 2 sts, *3 ch, dc (US sc) in next CL, 3 ch, dc (US sc) in next dc (US sc), repeat from * across to beginning chain, ending with dc (US sc) in top of beginning chain—10 x dc (US sc) + 7 x 3-ch sps.

Row 6: 1 ch, turn, dc (US sc) in first 2 sts, *3 ch, work CL in next dc (US sc), 3 ch, dc (US sc) in next dc (US sc), repeat from * across ending with tr (US dc) in each last 2 sts—3 x clusters + 5 x 3-ch sps + 2 x tr (US dc).

Subsequent rows: repeat rows 3 to 6 to desired size ending with row 3 or 5, then work 2 last rows as follows.

2nd last row: repeat row 3 or row 5.

Last row: 1 ch, turn, dc (US sc) in each st and 3 dc (US sc) in each 3-ch sp across—do not finish off—work 2 rounds of edging in working colour before finishing off.

Cluster/CL: (YO, insert hook in st indicated and draw up a loop, YO and draw through 2 loops) 4 times, YO and draw through all 5 loops on hook, 1 ch to close.

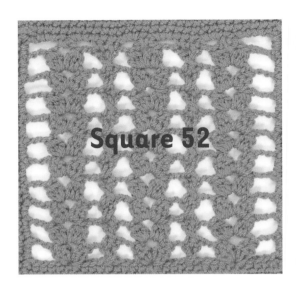

Square 52

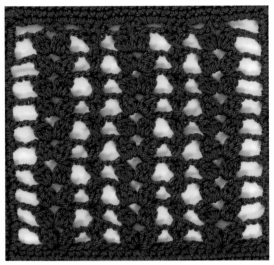

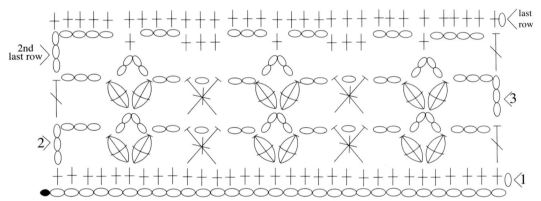

Foundation chain: With Col C make 32 ch.

Row 1: (right side) dc (US sc) in 2nd ch from hook and in each ch across—31 dc (US sc).

Row 2: 6 ch [count as tr (US dc) + 3-ch sp, now and throughout, beginning chain], turn, skip next 4 sts, *in next st work (CL, 4 ch, CL), 2 ch, skip next 5 sts, in next st work [tr (US dc), 1 ch], working backwards from st just made, skip next st, tr (US dc) in next st, working forward, 2 ch, skip next 3 sts, repeat from * across ending with 3 ch, skip 4 sts and tr (US dc) in last st—6 x clusters + 3 x 4-ch sps + 2 x cross sts.

Row 3: 6 ch, turn, *in next 4-ch sp work (CL, 4 ch, CL), 2 ch, skip next [tr (US dc), 1 ch], tr (US dc) in skipped st, 2 ch, repeat from * across ending with 3 ch and tr (US dc) in 3rd ch of beginning chain—6 x clusters + 3 x 4-ch sps + 2 x cross sts.

Subsequent rows: repeat row 3 to desired size, then work 2 last rows as follows.

2nd last row: 6 ch, turn, *dc (US sc) in next 4-ch sp, 3 ch, dc (US sc) in each next tr (US dc), 1-ch sp and tr (US dc), 3 ch, repeat from * across ending with 4 ch and tr (US dc) in 3rd ch of beginning chain—2 x 4-ch sps + 4 x 3-ch sps.

Last row: 1 ch, turn, dc (US sc) in first st, 4 dc (US sc) in next 4-ch sp, dc (US sc) in each st and 3 dc (US sc) in each 3-ch sp, across to last 4-ch sp, 4 dc (US sc) in last 4-ch sp and dc (US sc) in 3rd ch of beginning chain—do not finish off—work 2 rounds of edging in working colour before finishing off.

Cluster/CL: (YO, insert hook in st indicated and draw up a loop, YO and draw through 2 loops) 3 times, YO and draw through all 4 loops on hook.

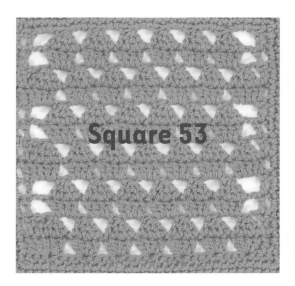

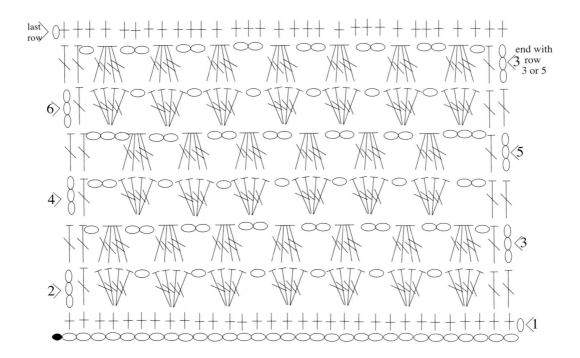

Foundation chain: With Col C make 32 ch.

Row 1: dc (US sc) in 2nd ch from hook and in each ch across—31 dc (US sc).

Row 2: (right side) 3 ch [count as tr (US dc) now and throughout, beginning chain], turn, tr (US dc) in next st, skip next st, *4 tr (US dc) in next st, 1 ch, skip 3 sts, repeat from * across ending with skip next st and tr (US dc) in each last 2 sts—7 x shells.

Row 3: 3 ch, turn, tr (US dc) in next st, 1 ch, *work CL over next 4 sts, 2 ch, repeat from * across ending with 1 ch, tr (US dc) in each last 2 sts—7 x clusters.

Row 4: 3 ch, turn, tr (US dc) in next st, 2 ch, *4 tr (US dc) in next 2-ch sp, 1 ch, repeat from * across ending with 2 ch and tr (US dc) in each last 2 sts—6 x shells.

Row 5: 3 ch, turn, tr (US dc) in next st, 3 ch, * work CL over next 4 sts, 2 ch, repeat from * across ending with 3 ch, tr (US dc) in each last 2 sts—6 x clusters.

Row 6: 3 ch, turn, tr (US dc) in next st, 4 tr (US dc) in next 3-ch sp, 1 ch, *4 tr (US dc) in next 2-ch sp, 1 ch, repeat from * across ending with 4 tr (US dc) in last 3-ch sp and tr (US dc) in each last 2 sts—7 x shells.

Subsequent rows: repeat rows 3 to 6 to desired size ending with row 3 or 5, then work last row as follows.

Last row: 1 ch, turn, dc (US sc) in each st, 1-ch sp and 3 dc (US sc) in each 2-ch or 3-ch sp across—do not finish off—work 2 rounds of edging in working colour before finishing off.

Cluster/CL: (YO, insert hook in st indicated and draw up a loop, YO and draw through 2 loops), repeat over number of sts indicated, YO and draw through all 5 loops on hook, 1 ch to close.

Square 54

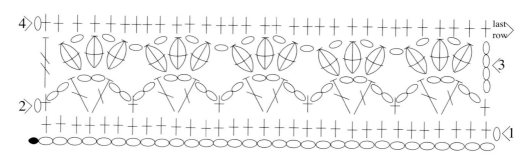

Foundation chain: With Col C make 32 ch.

Row 1: dc (US sc) in 2nd ch from hook and in each ch across—31 dc (US sc).

Row 2: (right side) 1 ch, turn, dc (US sc) in first st, *2 ch, skip next 2 sts, in next st work [tr (US dc), 2 ch, tr (US dc)] (V-st made), 2 ch, skip next 2 sts, dc (US sc) in next st, repeat from * across—15 x 2-ch sps.

Row 3: 4 ch [count as dtr (US tr) now and throughout, beginning chain], turn, *in next V-st work (CL, 1 ch) 3 times, repeat from * across to last V-st, then in last V-st work [(CL, 1 ch) twice + CL], ending with dtr (US tr) in last st—15 x clusters + 14 x 1-ch sps.

Row 4: 1 ch, turn, dc (US sc) in each st and 1-ch sp across—31 dc (US sc).

Subsequent rows: repeat rows 2 to 4 to desired size ending with row 4—do not finish off—work 2 rounds of edging in working colour before finishing off.

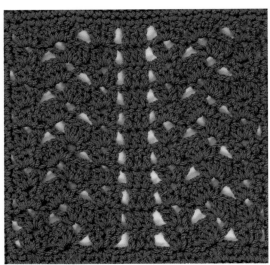 **Cluster/CL:** YO, insert hook in st indicated and draw up a loop, YO and draw through 2 loops) 3 times, YO and draw through all 4 loops on hook, 1 ch to close.

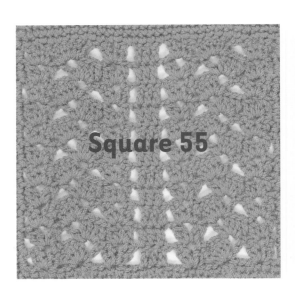

Square 55

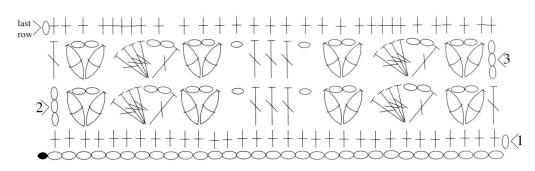

Foundation chain: With Col C make 32 ch.

Row 1: (right side) dc (US sc) in 2nd ch from hook and in each ch across—31 dc (US sc).

Row 2: 3 ch [count as tr (US dc) now and throughout, beginning chain], turn, skip next st, *in next st work (CL, 2 ch, CL), skip next 3 sts, in next st work [4 tr (US dc), 2 ch, tr (US dc)], skip next 3 sts, in next st work (CL, 2 ch, CL)**, 1 ch, skip next 3 sts, tr (US dc) in each next 3 sts, 1 ch, skip next 3 sts, repeat from * to ** once more, ending with skip next st and tr (US dc) in last st—8 x clusters + 6 x 2-ch sps + 5 x tr (US dc) + 2 x 1-ch sps.

Row 3: 3 ch, *in next 2-ch sp work (CL, 2 ch, CL), in next 2-ch sp work [4 tr (US dc), 2 ch, tr (US dc)], in next 2-ch sp work (CL, 2 ch, CL)**, 1 ch, tr (US dc) in each next 3 sts, 1 ch, repeat from * to ** once more, ending with tr (US dc) in last st—8 x clusters + 6 x 2-ch sps + 5 x tr (US dc) + 2 x 1-ch sps.

Subsequent rows: repeat row 3 to desired size, then work last row as follows.

Last row: 1 ch, turn, dc (US sc) in each st, 1-ch sp and 2-ch sp across—do not finish off—work 2 rounds of edging in working colour before finishing off.

Cluster/CL: YO, insert hook in st indicated and draw up a loop, YO and draw through 2 loops) twice, YO and draw through all 3 loops on hook.

Square 56

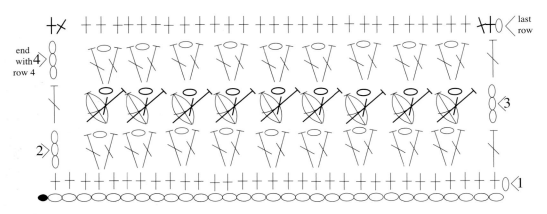

Foundation chain: With Col C make 32 ch.

Row 1: (right side) dc (US sc) in 2nd ch from hook and in each ch across—31 dc (US sc).

Row 2: 3 ch [count as tr (US dc) now and throughout, beginning chain], turn, *skip next 2 sts, in next st work [tr (US dc), 1 ch, tr (US dc)] (V-st made), repeat from * across ending with tr (US dc) in last st—9 x V-st.

Row 3: 3 ch, *work [tr (US dc), 1 ch] in 2nd tr (US dc) of next V-st, then working behind st just made, work CL in skipped tr (US dc) of same V-st, repeat from * across ending with tr (US dc) in top of beginning chain—9 x clusters + 11 x tr (US dc) + 9 x 1-ch sps.

Row 4: 3 ch, turn, *work V-st in next 1-ch sp, repeat from * across ending with tr (US dc) in last st—9 x V-st.

Subsequent rows: repeat rows 3 and 4 to desired size ending with row 4, then work last row as follows.

Last row: 1 ch, turn, 2 dc (US sc) in first st, dc (US sc) in each st and 1-ch sp across ending with 2 dc (US sc) in last st—do not finish off—work 2 rounds of edging in working colour before finishing off.

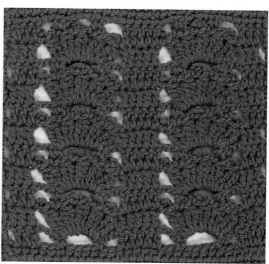 **Cluster/CL:** YO, insert hook in st indicated and draw up a loop, YO and draw through 2 loops) 3 times, YO and draw through all 4 loops on hook.

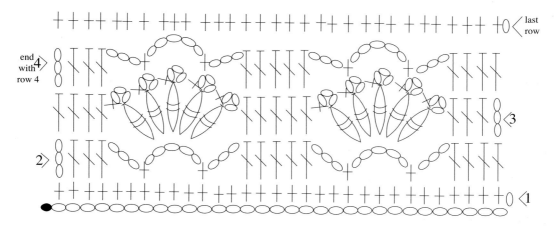

Foundation chain: With Col C make 32 ch.

Row 1: (right side) dc (US sc) in 2nd ch from hook and in each ch across—31 dc (US sc).

Row 2: 3 ch [count as tr (US dc) now and throughout, beginning chain], turn, tr (US dc) in next 3 sts, *3 ch, skip next 2 sts, dc (US sc) in next st, 5 ch, skip next 3 sts, dc (US sc) in next st, 3 ch, skip next 2 sts**, tr (US dc) in next 5 sts, repeat from * to ** ending with tr (US dc) in last 4 sts—13 x tr (US dc) + 2 x 5-ch sps + 4 x 3-ch sps.

Row 3: 3 ch, turn, tr (US dc) in next 3 sts, *work 5 picot-CL in next 5-ch sp, skip next 3-ch sp**, tr (US dc) in each next 5 sts, repeat from * to ** once more ending with tr (US dc) in each last 4 sts—13 x tr (US dc) + 10 x picot-cluster.

Row 4: 3 ch, turn, tr (US dc) in next 3 sts, *3 ch, skip next picot-CL, dc (US sc) in next picot, 5 ch, skip next picot-CL, dc (US sc) in next picot, 3 ch**, tr (US dc) in each next 5 tr (US dc), repeat from * to ** once more ending with tr (US dc) in each last 4 sts—13 x tr (US dc) + 2 x 5-ch sps + 4 x 3-ch sps.

Subsequent rows: repeat rows 3 and 4 to desired size ending with row 4, then work last row as follows.

Last row: 1 ch, turn, dc (US sc) in each st, 2 dc (US sc) in each 3-ch sp across and 3 dc (US sc) in each 5-ch sp—do not finish off—work 2 rounds of edging in working colour before finishing off.

Picot-cluster/picot-CL: (YO twice, insert hook into st indicated and draw up a loop, YO and draw through 2 loops, twice) 2 times, YO and draw through all 3 loops on hook (cluster made), 3 ch, dc (US sc) in top of cluster just made (picot made)—picot-cluster made.

Square 58

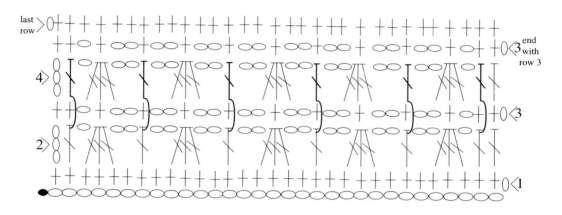

Foundation chain: With Col C make 32 ch.

Row 1: dc (US sc) in 2nd ch from hook and in each ch across—31 dc (US sc).

Row 2: (right side) 3 ch [count as tr (US dc) now and throughout, beginning chain], turn, tr (US dc) in next st, 1 ch, *work CL over next 3 st, 2 ch, skip next st, tr (US dc) in next st, 2 ch, skip next st, repeat from * across ending with 1 ch, tr (US dc) in each last 2 sts—5 x

clusters + 2 x 1-ch sps + 8 x 2-ch sps + 8 x tr (US dc).

Row 3: 1 ch, turn, dc (US sc) in first 2 sts, 1 ch, *dc (US sc) in next CL, 2 ch, dc (US sc) in next tr (US dc), 2 ch, repeat from * across ending with 1 ch, dc (US sc) in each last 2 sts—2 x 1-ch sps + 8 x 2-ch sps + 13 x dc (US sc).

Row 4: (work FP sts loosely) 3 ch, FPtr (US FPdc) around next st 2 rows below, 1 ch, work CL [over next 1-ch sp, in next dc (US sc), over first ch of next 2-ch sp], *2 ch, FPtr (US FPdc) around next st 2 rows below, 2 ch, work CL [over last ch of next 2-ch sp, in next dc (US sc), over first ch of next 2-ch sp], repeat from * across ending with work CL [over last ch of next 2-ch sp, in next dc (US sc), over 1-ch sp], 1 ch, FPtr (US FPdc) around next st 2 rows below, tr (US dc) in last st—5 x clusters + 2 x 1-ch sps + 8 x 2-ch sps + 6 x FPtr (US FPdc) + 2 x tr (US dc).

Row 5: 1 ch, turn, dc (US sc) in first 2 sts, 1 ch, *dc (US sc) in next CL, 2 ch, dc (US sc) in next FPtr (US FPdc), 2 ch, repeat from * across ending with 1 ch, dc (US sc) in each last 2 sts—2 x 1-ch sps + 8 x 2-ch sps + 13 x dc (US sc).

Subsequent rows: repeat rows 4 and 5 to desired size ending with row 5, then work last row as follows

Last row: 1 ch, turn, dc (US sc) in each st and 1-ch sp, 2 dc (US sc) in each 2-ch sp across—do not finish off—work 2 rounds of edging in working colour before finishing off.

Front post treble/FPtr (US front post double crochet/FPdc): YO, insert hook from front to back around post of stitch indicated, (YO and draw through 2 loops) twice.

Cluster/CL: YO, insert hook in or over st indicated and draw up a loop, YO and draw through 2 loops), repeat over number of sts indicated, YO and draw through all 4 loops on hook.

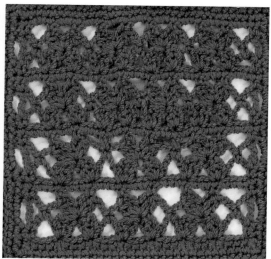

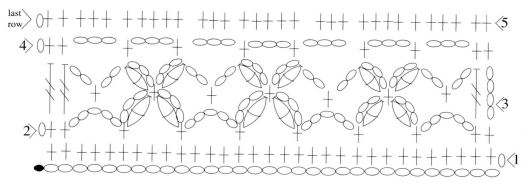

Foundation chain: With Col C make 32 ch.

Row 1: (right side) dc (US sc) in 2nd ch from hook and in each ch across—31 dc (US sc).

Row 2: 1 ch, turn, dc (US sc) in first 2 sts, *5 ch, skip next 3 sts, in next st work [dc (US sc), 3 ch, CL] skip next 3 sts, in next st work [CL, 3 ch, dc (US sc)], repeat from * across ending with 5 ch, dc (US sc) in each last 2 sts—4 x 5-ch sps + 6 x clusters.

Row 3: 4 ch [count as dtr (US tr) now and throughout, beginning chain], turn, dtr (US tr) in next st, *2 ch, dc (US sc) in next 5-ch sp, 2 ch, in centre between next 2 CLs work [CL, 3 ch, dc (US sc), 3ch, CL], repeat from * across ending with dtr (US tr) in each last 2 sts—8 x 2-ch sps + 6 x clusters.

Row 4: 1 ch, turn, dc (US sc) in first 2 sts, *3 ch, dc (US sc) in next CL (in top of 3-ch), 3 ch, dc (US sc) in next CL (in top of 3 ch), repeat from * across ending with dc (US sc) in each last 2 sts—7 x 3-ch sps.

Row 5: 1 ch, turn, dc (US sc) in each st and 3 dc (US sc) in each 3-ch sp across—31 dc (US sc)

Subsequent rows: repeat rows 2 to 5 to desired size ending with row 5—do not finish off—work 2 rounds of edging in working colour before finishing off.

Cluster/CL: (YO, insert hook in st indicated and draw up a loop, YO and draw through 2 loops) twice, YO and draw through all 3 loops on hook.

Square 60

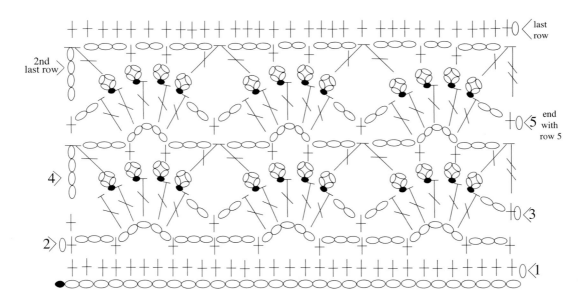

Foundation chain: With Col C make 32 ch.

Row 1: (right side) dc (US sc) in 2nd ch from hook and in each ch across—31 dc (US sc).

Row 2: 1 ch, turn, dc (US sc) in first st, 3 ch, skip next 2 sts, dc (US sc) in next st, *5 ch, skip next 3 sts, [dc (US sc) in next st, skip 3 ch, 2 sts] twice, dc (US sc) in next st, repeat from * across ending with 3 ch, skip next 2 sts and dc (US sc) in last st—6 x 3-ch sps + 3 x 5-ch sps.

Row 3: 1 ch, turn, dc (US sc) in first st, *2 ch, skip next 3-ch sp, in next 5-ch sp work [{tr (US dc), picot} 4 times, tr (US dc)] (shell made), 2 ch, skip next 3-ch sp, dc (US sc) in next dc (US sc), repeat from * across ending with 2 ch, skip 3-ch sp and dc (US sc) in last st—3 x shells.

Row 4: 4 ch, turn, tr (US dc) in next picot [count 4 ch and tr (US dc) just made as BCL], *3 ch, dc (US sc) in next picot, 5 ch, dc (US sc) in next picot, 3 ch, work CL over next 2 picots, repeat from * across ending with 3 ch, work ECL over last picot and last st—1 x BCL + 6 x 3-ch sps + 6 x dc (US sc) + 3 x 5-ch sps + 2 x CL + 1 x ECL.

Row 5: 1 ch, turn, dc (US sc) in first st, *2 ch, work shell in next 5-ch sp, 2 ch, dc (US sc) in next CL, repeat from * across ending with dc (US sc) in last BCL.

Subsequent rows: repeat rows 4 and 5 to desired size ending with row 5, then work 2 last rows as follows.

2nd last row: 4 ch, turn, tr (US dc) in next picot, *3 ch, dc (US sc) in next picot, 2 ch, dc (US sc) in next picot, 3 ch, work CL over next 2 picots, repeat from * across ending with 3 ch, ECL in last st.

Last row: 1 ch, turn, dc (US sc) in each st and in each 2-ch sp, 3 dc (US sc) in each 3-ch sp across—do not finish off—work 2 rounds of edging in working colour before finishing off.

Cluster/CL: YO, insert hook in st and draw up a loop, YO and draw through 2 loops), repeat over number of sts indicated, YO and draw through 3 loops on hook.

Beginning cluster/BCL: Count 4 ch and tr (US dc) just made as BCL.

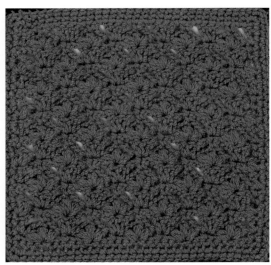

End cluster/ECL: [(YO, insert hook in st indicated and draw up a loop, YO and draw through 2 loops), YO twice, insert hook in next st indicated and draw up a loop, YO and draw through 2 loops twice], YO and draw through 3 loops on hook—end cluster made.

Picot: 4 ch, ss in 4th ch from hook (for best results work picot tightly)

Square 61

Foundation chain: With Col C make 32 ch.

Row 1: dc (US sc) in 2nd ch from hook and in each ch across—31 dc (US sc).

Row 2: (right side) 1 ch, turn, dc (US sc) in first st, *skip 2 sts, in next st work (puff, 2 ch, puff, 2 ch, puff), 1 ch, skip 2 sts, dc (US sc) in next st, repeat from * across—5 x 3-puff groups.

Row 3: 3 ch [count as tr (US dc) now and throughout, beginning chain], turn, tr (US dc) in same st, 2 ch, *dc (US sc) in 2nd puff of 3-puff group, 2 ch, 3 tr (US dc) in next dc (US sc), 2 ch, repeat from * across ending with 2 tr (US dc) in last st—10 x 2-ch sps.

Row 4: 4 ch [count as tr (US dc) + 1 ch now and throughout, beginning chain], turn, puff in same st, *1 ch, dc (US sc) in next dc (US sc), in 2nd st of next 3-tr (US dc) group work (puff, 2 ch, puff, 2 ch, puff), repeat from * across to beginning chain, ending with skip next tr (US dc) then work [puff, 2 ch, tr (US dc)] in top of beginning chain—4 x 3-puff groups.

Row 5: 1 ch, turn, dc (US sc) in first st, *2 ch, 3 tr (US dc) in next dc (US sc), 2 ch, dc (US sc) in 2nd puff of 3-puff group, 2 ch, repeat from * across to beginning chain, dc (US sc) in 3rd ch of beginning chain.

Row 6: 1 ch, turn, dc (US sc) in first st, *in 2nd st of next 3-tr (US dc) group work (puff, 2 ch, puff, 2 ch, puff), 1 ch, dc (US sc) in next st, repeat from * across—5 x 3-puff groups.

Subsequent rows: repeat rows 3 to 6 to desired size ending with row 3 or row 5, then work last row as follows.

Last row: 1 ch, turn, dc (US sc) in each st and 2-ch sp across—do not finish off—work 2 rounds of edging in working colour before finishing off.

Puff st: In st indicated work (YO and draw up a loop) twice (5 loops on hook), YO and draw through all 5 loops—puff made.

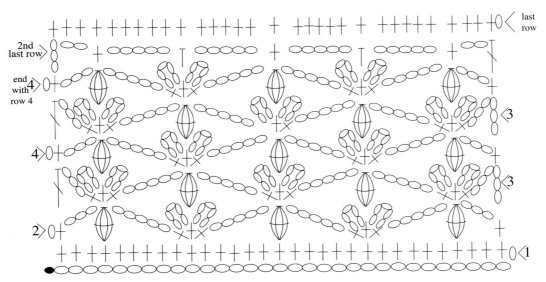

Foundation chain: With Col C make 32 ch.

Row 1: (right side) dc (US sc) in 2nd ch from hook and in each ch across—31 dc (US sc).

Row 2: 1 ch, turn, dc (US sc) in first st, 3 ch, skip next 2 sts, *CL in next st, 5 ch, skip next 5 sts, in next st work [dc (US sc), 5ch, dc (US sc), 5 ch, dc (US sc)], 5 ch, skip next 5 sts, repeat from * across ending with 3 ch, skip 2 sts and dc (US sc) in last st—3 x CL + 2 x dc (US sc)-5-ch groups.

Row 3: 6 ch [count as tr (US dc) + 3 ch, now and throughout, beginning chain], turn, *in next CL work [dc (US sc), 5ch, dc (US sc), 5 ch, dc (US sc)], 5 ch, CL in centre st of next dc (US sc)-5-ch group, 5 ch, repeat from * across ending with 3 ch and tr (US dc) in last st—2 x CL + 3 x dc (US sc)-5-ch groups.

Row 4: 1 ch, turn, dc (US sc) in first st, 3 ch, *CL in centre st of next dc (US sc)-5-ch group, 5 ch, in next CL work [dc (US sc), 5 ch, dc (US sc), 5 ch, dc (US sc)], 5 ch, repeat from * across ending with 3 ch and dc (US sc) in 3rd ch of beginning chain—3 x clusters + 2 x dc (US sc)-5-ch groups.

Subsequent rows: repeat rows 3 and 4 to desired size ending with row 4, then work 2 last rows as follows.

2nd last row: 5 ch [count as tr (US dc) + 2 ch], turn, *dc (US sc) in next CL, 5 ch,

htr (US hdc) in centre st of next dc (US sc)-5-ch group, 5 ch, repeat from * across ending with 2 ch and tr (US dc) in last st—4 x 5-ch sps + 2 x 2-ch sps.

Last row: 1 ch, turn, dc (US sc) in each st and 2 dc (US sc) in each 2-ch sp and 5 dc (US sc) in each 5-ch sp ending with dc (US sc) in 3rd ch of beginning chain across—do not finish off—work 2 rounds of edging in working colour before finishing off.

Cluster/CL: (YO, insert hook in st indicated and draw up a loop, YO and draw through 2 loops) 4 times, YO and draw through all 5 loops on hook, 1 ch to close.

Square 63

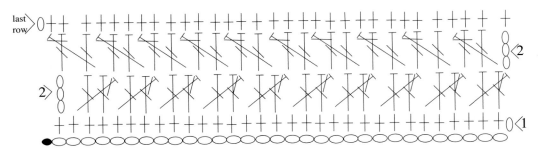

Foundation chain: With Col C make 32 ch.

Row 1: (right side) dc (US sc) in 2nd ch from hook and in each ch across—31 dc (US sc).

Row 2: 3 ch [count as tr (US dc) now and throughout, beginning chain], turn, work slant st across—10 x slant sts.

Subsequent rows: repeat row 2 to desired size, then work last row as follows.

Last row: 1 ch, turn, dc (US sc) in each st across—do not finish off—work 2 rounds of edging in working colour before finishing off.

Slant stitch: Skip next st, tr (US dc) in each next 2 sts, working over 2 sts just made work Ltr (US Ldc) in skipped st.

Long treble/Ltr (US long double crochet/Ldc): (YO, insert hook in st indicated and draw up a loop level with working sts just made, YO and draw through 2 loops twice.

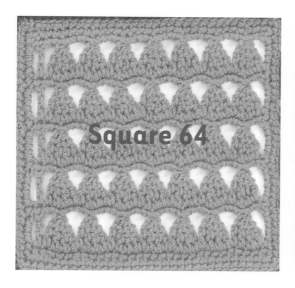

Square 64

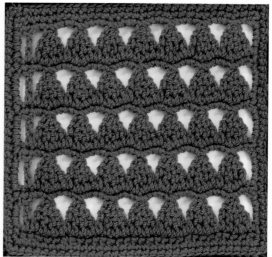

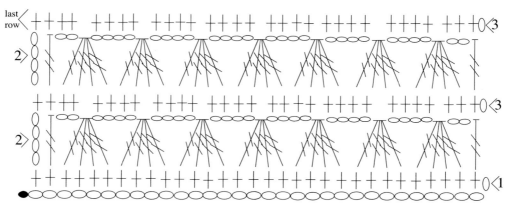

Foundation chain: With Col C make 32 ch.

Row 1: (right side) dc (US sc) in 2nd ch from hook and in each ch across—31 dc (US sc).

Row 2: 4 ch [count as dtr (US tr), now and throughout, beginning chain], turn, dtr (US tr) in next st, 2 ch, *work CL over next 4 sts, 4 ch, repeat from * across ending with 2 ch and dtr (US tr) in last st—7 x clusters.

Row 3: 1 ch, turn, dc (US sc) in first st, 2 dc (US sc) in next 2-ch sp, *skip CL, 4 dc (US sc) in next 4-ch sp, repeat from * across ending with 2 ch and dtr (US tr) in each last 2 sts—31 dc (US sc).

Subsequent rows: repeat rows 2 and 3 to desired size ending with row 3—do not finish off—work 2 rounds of edging in working colour before finishing off.

Double treble/dtr (US treble/tr): YO twice, insert hook in st or sp and pull up a loop, YO and draw through 2 loops on hook 3 times.

Cluster/CL: (YO twice, insert hook in st indicated and draw up a loop, YO and draw through 2 loops twice,) repeat over number of sts indicated, YO and draw through all 5 loops on hook.

CHECKLIST

Colour group A

- ❑ No 1
- ❑ No 2
- ❑ No 3
- ❑ No 4
- ❑ No 5
- ❑ No 6
- ❑ No 7
- ❑ No 8
- ❑ No 9
- ❑ No 10
- ❑ No 11
- ❑ No 12
- ❑ No 13
- ❑ No 14
- ❑ No 15
- ❑ No 16

- ❑ No 17
- ❑ No 18
- ❑ No 19
- ❑ No 20
- ❑ No 21
- ❑ No 22

Colour group B

- ❑ No 23
- ❑ No 24
- ❑ No 25
- ❑ No 26
- ❑ No 27
- ❑ No 28
- ❑ No 29
- ❑ No 30
- ❑ No 31
- ❑ No 32

- ❑ No 33
- ❑ No 34
- ❑ No 35
- ❑ No 36
- ❑ No 37
- ❑ No 38
- ❑ No 39
- ❑ No 40
- ❑ No 41
- ❑ No 42
- ❑ No 43

Colour group C

- ❑ No 44
- ❑ No 45
- ❑ No 46
- ❑ No 47
- ❑ No 48

- ❑ No 49
- ❑ No 50
- ❑ No 51
- ❑ No 52
- ❑ No 53
- ❑ No 54
- ❑ No 55
- ❑ No 56
- ❑ No 57
- ❑ No 58
- ❑ No 59
- ❑ No 60
- ❑ No 61
- ❑ No 62
- ❑ No 63
- ❑ No 64

Supplier

Bendigo Woollen Mills

4 Lansell Street, Bendigo

VIC 3550

ph: + 61 03 5442 4600

fax: + 61 03 5442 2918

www.bendigowoollenmills.com.au